CALEB ROSS

Go Programming For Absolute Beginners

Copyright © 2024 by Caleb Ross

All rights reserved. No part of this publication may be reproduced, stored or transmitted in any form or by any means, electronic, mechanical, photocopying, recording, scanning, or otherwise without written permission from the publisher. It is illegal to copy this book, post it to a website, or distribute it by any other means without permission.

First edition

This book was professionally typeset on Reedsy.
Find out more at reedsy.com

Contents

Preface	1
Section I: Getting Started with Go ...	5
Chapter 2: Go Basics	12
Chapter 3: Functions and Packages	23
Chapter 4: Structs and Interfaces	32
Section II: Building Real-World Applications Chapter 5:...	40
Chapter 7: Concurrent Programming	50
Chapter 8: Working with Databases	62
Section III: Leveling Up Your Go Skills ...	78
Chapter 10: Debugging and Error Handling	91
Chapter 11: Advanced Language Features	101
Chapter 12: Deploying Go Applications	112
Section IV: Go in the Real World ...	123
Chapter 14: Go Best Practices and Idioms	128
Conclusion: The Go Community and Ecosystem	140

Preface

Welcome to "Go Programming for Absolute Beginners"! If you're picking up this book, chances are you've heard about the Go programming language and are curious to learn more. Maybe you're a complete newcomer to programming, or perhaps you have some coding experience but are looking to add Go to your skill set. Either way, you've come to the right place.

Who This Book Is For

This book is designed specifically for absolute beginners who have little to no prior programming experience. If you've never written a line of code before, don't worry – we'll guide you through everything you need to know, step by step. You don't need any fancy degrees or prerequisites, just a computer, an internet connection, and a willingness to learn.

That being said, this book can also be valuable for readers who have some familiarity with other programming languages. Go has its own unique features and conventions, so even experienced developers can benefit from a thorough introduction to the language.

Regardless of your background, our goal is to make learning Go as accessible and enjoyable as possible. We'll start from the very beginning and gradually build up your skills, so you can work through the book at your own pace.

What You Will Learn

By the end of this book, you'll have a solid foundation in Go programming and be able to build your own real-world applications. Here's a preview of some of the key things you'll learn:

- How to install Go and set up your development environment
- The fundamental concepts of Go, including variables, data types, control structures, and functions
- How to organize your code with packages and modules
- Working with essential data structures like arrays, slices, and maps
- Defining your own custom types with structs and interfaces
- Handling errors and writing robust, reliable code
- Using Go's powerful concurrency features to write efficient, parallel programs
- Interacting with files, databases, and external APIs
- Creating command-line tools and web applications
- Testing, debugging, and profiling your Go programs
- Deploying your applications to the cloud
- Best practices and idiomatic patterns for writing clean, maintainable Go code

In addition to teaching you the language itself, we'll also focus on the practical skills you need to be a productive Go programmer. You'll work through multiple hands-on projects that reinforce your learning and give you experience building real applications. By the time you finish this book, you'll have a portfolio of working code samples to showcase your new skills.

We'll also go beyond just the basics of the language. You'll learn about the wider Go ecosystem, including important libraries and frameworks, and how to engage with the vibrant community of Go developers worldwide. We've even included interviews with seasoned Go experts who share their insights and advice for succeeding with the language.

How This Book Is Structured

This book is divided into four main sections, each focusing on a different aspect of learning Go:

1. **Getting Started with Go**: In this section, we'll introduce you to the Go programming language and help you get your development environment set up. You'll write your first Go programs and learn about essential language features like variables, data types, functions, and control structures.
2. **Building Real-World Applications**: Here's where things get really exciting – you'll dive into building actual Go applications, increasing in complexity from command-line tools to web servers to database-driven APIs. Along the way, you'll explore key concepts like file I/O, error handling, goroutines, and more.
3. **Leveling Up Your Go Skills**: In this section, you'll graduate from Go novice to pro. We'll cover advanced topics like testing, debugging, performance optimization, and deployment that will help you write high-quality, production-ready code. You'll also learn about some of Go's more powerful features like reflection and unsafe code.
4. **Go in the Real World**: The final section of the book connects you with the broader Go community. We'll share insights from expert Go developers, guide you through best practices and idiomatic Go patterns, and introduce you to the wealth of libraries and resources available to Go programmers.

Each chapter is structured to make learning easy, with clear explanations, illustrative diagrams, and working code samples. At the end of each chapter, you'll find exercises to test your knowledge and challenge you to experiment further with your newly acquired skills.

We've also included handy reference materials like cheat sheets and a quick-lookup index, so you can easily refresh your memory or find the information you need.

Whether you read this book cover-to-cover or dip in to specific topics, you'll find a wealth of practical, hands-on guidance to learning Go. So let's dive in and start your journey to becoming a confident, capable Go programmer!

Section I: Getting Started with Go
Chapter 1: Introduction to Go Programming

Welcome to the exciting world of Go programming! In this section, we'll introduce you to the Go language, explore what makes it special, and help you get your development environment set up so you can start writing your first Go programs.

Chapter 1: Introduction to Go Programming

Before we dive into the specifics of the Go language, let's take a step back and look at the bigger picture. What exactly is Go, and why has it become so popular in recent years?

What is Go?

Go, also known as Golang, is a modern, open-source programming language developed by Google. It was first released in 2009, with the goal of creating a language that combined the ease of programming of an interpreted, dynamically-typed language like Python with the efficiency and safety of a statically-typed, compiled language like C++.

At its core, Go is a compiled, statically-typed language with syntax loosely derived from C. However, it also includes a number of features that make it feel more like a dynamic language, such as built-in concurrency support, garbage collection, and a powerful standard library.

Some of the key characteristics of Go include:

- **Simplicity**: Go has a clean, minimal syntax that is easy to read and write. It eschews many of the complex features of other languages in favor of a smaller, more orthogonal feature set.
- **Strong and static typing**: Every variable in Go has a specific type, which is checked at compile time. This catches many common errors early in the development process.
- **Compiled**: Go code is compiled to native machine code, which means it executes very efficiently.
- **Garbage-collected**: Go has automatic memory management, so developers don't need to manually allocate and free memory.
- **Concurrent**: Go has built-in support for concurrency through goroutines and channels, making it easy to write parallel and asynchronous code.
- **Batteries included**: Go comes with a comprehensive standard library that covers everything from I/O to cryptography to JSON parsing, reducing the need for third-party dependencies.

These features combine to make Go a powerful, efficient, and enjoyable language to work with, suitable for a wide range of applications from system programming to web development to data analysis.

Why Learn Go?

So why should you learn Go? Whether you're a seasoned developer or completely new to programming, there are many compelling reasons to add Go to your toolkit:

1. **It's in high demand**: Many companies, from startups to large enter-

prises, are adopting Go for its performance, simplicity, and scalability. Learning Go can open up exciting job opportunities.
2. **It's fast and efficient**: Go programs compile to native machine code and execute very efficiently, making it an excellent choice for systems programming, web servers, and other performance-critical applications.
3. **It's easy to learn**: Go has a clean, minimal syntax that is quick to learn, especially if you already have experience with a C-like language. Even if you're new to programming, Go's simplicity makes it a great first language.
4. **It has excellent tooling**: Go comes with a powerful set of tools for testing, profiling, debugging, and managing dependencies, which make developing large, complex applications much easier.
5. **It's fun!**: Many developers find Go's simplicity and elegance refreshing and enjoyable to work with. Its built-in concurrency features and powerful standard library make it a pleasure to use for a wide range of tasks.

Whether you're looking to boost your career, improve your programming skills, or just learn something new and exciting, Go is definitely worth your time.

Advantages of Go

Let's dive a bit deeper into some of the key advantages that set Go apart from other programming languages:

1. **Simplicity and readability**: Go's syntax is designed to be clean, concise, and easy to understand. It avoids many of the complex features of other languages, such as inheritance and generics, in favor of a smaller, more orthogonal feature set. This makes Go code easier to read, write, and maintain, even for large codebases.
2. **Fast compilation**: Go's compiler is incredibly fast, with build times often measured in seconds rather than minutes. This rapid feedback

loop makes development much more efficient and enjoyable.
3. **Excellent performance**: Go programs are compiled to native machine code and execute very efficiently, often approaching the speed of C or C++. This makes Go an excellent choice for system programming, web servers, and other performance-critical applications.
4. **Built-in concurrency**: Go has concurrency primitives built directly into the language, in the form of goroutines (lightweight threads) and channels (for communication between goroutines). This makes it very easy to write concurrent and parallel programs, without the need for complex synchronization mechanisms.
5. **Garbage collection**: Unlike languages like C or C++, Go has automatic memory management through garbage collection. This frees developers from the burden of manually allocating and freeing memory, and eliminates a whole class of memory-related bugs.
6. **Rich standard library**: Go comes with a comprehensive standard library that provides high-quality implementations of many common programming tasks, from HTTP servers to JSON parsing to cryptography. This reduces the need for third-party dependencies and makes it easier to write portable, self-contained applications.
7. **Cross-platform compilation**: Go programs can be compiled for a wide range of operating systems and architectures, from Linux to Windows to macOS, and from 32-bit to 64-bit processors. This makes it easy to write portable code that can run almost anywhere.
8. **Robust tooling**: Go comes with a powerful set of tools for testing, profiling, debugging, formatting, and managing dependencies. These tools are well-integrated with the language and make it easier to write high-quality, maintainable code.
9. **Vibrant community**: Go has a thriving ecosystem of developers, libraries, and tools. The community is known for being welcoming and helpful to newcomers, with many high-quality learning resources and open-source projects available.

These advantages, combined with Go's increasing adoption in industry, make it a compelling language to learn for both beginners and experienced developers alike.

Installing Go and Setting Up Your Environment

Now that you're excited about learning Go, let's get your development environment set up! The process is fairly straightforward and should only take a few minutes.

1. **Download Go**: First, visit the official Go downloads page at https://golang.org/dl/. Here, you'll find installers for Windows, macOS, and Linux. Choose the package appropriate for your operating system and download it.
2. **Install Go**: Once the download is complete, run the installer. Follow the prompts, choosing the default installation options unless you have specific needs. The installer will set up the Go distribution and associated tools.
3. **Check the installation**: Open a command prompt or terminal and type go version. You should see output similar to go version go1.16.4 darwin/amd64, indicating a successful installation.
4. **Set up your workspace**: Go expects your code to be organized in a specific way, with a single workspace directory containing three subdirectories:

- src: Contains Go source files organized into packages.
- pkg: Contains compiled package objects.
- bin: Contains compiled executable programs.

1. Create a directory for your Go workspace, for example, go-projects, and within it create the three subdirectories.
2. **Configure environment variables**: Go relies on two environment variables to find your code:

- GOROOT: This points to the directory where Go is installed. The installer typically sets this automatically.
- GOPATH: This points to your Go workspace directory.

1. Set GOPATH to the path of your go-projects directory. The process for doing this varies by operating system, but typically involves editing your shell profile file (e.g., .bash_profile on macOS or Linux) or using the System Properties dialog on Windows.
2. **Choose an editor or IDE**: While Go code can be written in any text editor, an integrated development environment (IDE) can provide features like code completion, debugging, and refactoring. Some popular choices for Go development include:

- VSCode with the Go extension
- GoLand (commercial)
- Vim with Go plugins

1. Choose the editor that best fits your needs and preferences.
2. **Write your first program**: To verify your setup, create a simple "Hello, World!" program. In your src directory, create a hello directory, and within it create a file named hello.go with the following contents:

```go
Copy
package main

import "fmt"

func main() {
    fmt.Println("Hello, World!")
}
```

1. From your workspace directory, run the program with go run src/hel-

SECTION I: GETTING STARTED WITH GO ...

lo/hello.go. You should see Hello, World! printed to the console.

Congratulations! You now have a working Go development environment. In the next chapter, we'll start exploring the fundamentals of the Go language itself.

Chapter 2: Go Basics

Now that you have your Go development environment set up, it's time to start exploring the fundamentals of the language. In this chapter, we'll cover the basic building blocks of Go programs, from the structure of the workspace to the syntax for variables, types, expressions, and control flow.

The Go Workspace

Before we dive into the details of the Go language, let's take a closer look at how Go projects are organized. As mentioned in the previous chapter, Go expects your code to be structured in a specific way, with a single workspace directory containing three subdirectories:

- src: This is where your Go source files live. They are organized into packages, with each package in its own directory. For example, the source files for a hello package would be in src/hello.
- pkg: This directory contains compiled package objects. When you build a package, the compiled output is stored here, in a subdirectory corresponding to your operating system and architecture (e.g., darwin_amd64 for 64-bit macOS).
- bin: This directory contains compiled executable programs. When you build a main package (a package that can be executed directly), the

resulting binary is stored here.

The GOPATH environment variable points to the root of your workspace directory. When you import packages in your Go code, the compiler looks for them in the src directory of your GOPATH.

It's possible to have multiple workspaces by setting GOPATH to a list of directories, but it's generally recommended to have a single workspace for all your Go projects.

Writing Your First Go Program

Now let's write a simple Go program to print "Hello, World!" to the console. Create a new directory named hello inside your src directory, and within it create a file named hello.go with the following contents:

```go
Copy
package main

import "fmt"

func main() {
    fmt.Println("Hello, World!")
}
```

Let's break this down line by line:

- package main: Every Go source file starts with a package declaration. The main package is special - it defines an executable program, as opposed to a library.
- import "fmt": This line imports the fmt package, which provides functions for formatted I/O (input/output). Imported packages are searched for in the src directory of your GOPATH.
- func main() { ... }: The main function is the entry point of an executable program. It takes no arguments and returns no values.

- fmt.Println("Hello, World!"): This line calls the Println function from the fmt package, which prints its arguments to the console followed by a newline.

To run this program, open a terminal, navigate to your workspace directory, and run:

```
Copy
go run src/hello/hello.go
```

You should see Hello, World! printed to the console.

Alternatively, you can build the program into an executable binary with:

```
Copy
go build src/hello/hello.go
```

This will create an executable named hello (or hello.exe on Windows) in your workspace directory, which you can then run with ./hello.

Variables and Constants

Variables in Go are declared with the var keyword, followed by the variable name, type, and an optional initial value. For example:

```go
Copy
var x int
var y int = 7
var z = 8
```

If an initial value is provided, the type can be omitted - the variable will take the type of the initializer. If no initial value is provided, the variable is initialized to the zero value for its type (0 for numbers, false for booleans, "" for strings).

Variables declared without an initial value are initialized to their zero values:

```go
var a int    // 0
var b bool   // false
var c string // ""
```

You can also declare multiple variables at once:

```go
var a, b int = 1, 2
var c, d = 3, "four"
```

Within a function, the := short assignment statement can be used in place of a var declaration with implicit type:

```go
func main() {
    x := 5
    y := "hello"
    z := true
}
```

Constants are declared with the const keyword. They can be character, string, boolean, or numeric values. Numeric constants can be given a specific type or left untyped:

```go
const Pi = 3.14
const (
    StatusOK = 200
```

```
    StatusCreated = 201
    StatusAccepted = 202
)
```

Data Types

Go is a statically-typed language, which means that every variable has a type that is known at compile time. Go has several built-in types:

- **Boolean**: bool represents a boolean value, either true or false.
- **Numeric types**:
- **Integers**: Signed integers (int, int8, int16, int32, int64) and unsigned integers (uint, uint8, uint16, uint32, uint64). The int and uint types are usually 32 bits wide on 32-bit systems and 64 bits wide on 64-bit systems.
- **Floating-point**: float32 and float64 represent IEEE-754 floating-point numbers.
- **Complex numbers**: complex64 and complex128 represent complex numbers with float32 and float64 real and imaginary parts.
- **String**: string represents a string of Unicode characters. Strings are immutable in Go.
- **Array**: An array is a numbered sequence of elements of a single type with a fixed length. The type [n]T is an array of n values of type T:

```go
Copy
var a [10]int
```

- **Slice**: A slice is a dynamically-sized, flexible view into the elements of an array. The type []T is a slice with elements of type T:

```go
Copy
var s []int = a[1:4]
```

- **Map**: A map is an unordered group of elements of one type, called the element type, indexed by a set of unique keys of another type, called the key type. The type map[K]T is a map with keys of type K and values of type T:

```go
Copy
var m map[string]int
```

- **Pointer**: A pointer holds the memory address of a value. The type *T is a pointer to a T value:

```go
Copy
var p *int
```

- **Function**: A function type denotes the set of all functions with the same parameter and result types:

```go
Copy
```

```go
var f func(a, b int) int
```

- **Interface**: An interface type is defined as a set of method signatures. A value of interface type can hold any value that implements those methods:

```go
Copy
type Reader interface {
    Read(p []byte) (n int, err error)
}
```

- **Struct**: A struct is a collection of fields:

```go
Copy
type Person struct {
    Name string
    Age  int
}
```

These are the fundamental types in Go. We'll explore many of them in more detail throughout this book.

Operators and Expressions

Go supports the usual arithmetic operators (+, -, *, /, %), as well as increment and decrement operators (++, —). These can be used to form arithmetic expressions:

CHAPTER 2: GO BASICS

```go
x := 5
y := 3
z := (x + y) * 2
```

Comparison operators (==, !=, <, <=, >, >=) compare two values and yield a boolean:

```go
x := 5
y := 3
z := x > y  // z is true
```

Logical operators (&&, ||, !) operate on boolean values:

```go
x := true
y := false
z := x && !y  // z is true
```

Bitwise operators (&, |, ^, «, ») operate on integers:

```go
var x uint8 = 0b00101010
var y uint8 = 0b00001111
z := x & y  // z is 0b00001010
```

Assignment operators (=, +=, -=, *=, /=, %=, «=, »=, &=, ^=, |=) assign values to variables:

```go
x := 5
x += 3  // x is now 8
```

Control Flow Statements

Go provides several statements for controlling the flow of execution in a program:

- if statements:

```go
if x > 5 {
    fmt.Println("x is greater than 5")
} else if x < 5 {
    fmt.Println("x is less than 5")
} else {
    fmt.Println("x is equal to 5")
}
```

- for loops:

```go
for i := 0; i < 5; i++ {
    fmt.Println(i)
}
```

- while loops (using for):

```go
Copy
i := 0
for i < 5 {
    fmt.Println(i)
    i++
}
```

- switch statements:

```go
Copy
switch day {
case "Mon", "Tue", "Wed", "Thu", "Fri":
    fmt.Println("Weekday")
case "Sat", "Sun":
    fmt.Println("Weekend")
default:
    fmt.Println("Invalid day")
}
```

- Labeled break and continue statements:

```go
Copy
outer:
for i := 0; i < 5; i++ {
    for j := 0; j < 5; j++ {
        if j == 3 {
            continue outer
        }
        fmt.Println(i, j)
```

        }
}

- defer statements (deferred until surrounding function returns):

```go
Copy
func main() {
    defer fmt.Println("world")
    fmt.Println("hello")
}
```

These control flow mechanisms, combined with the basic types and syntax we've covered, provide the foundation for writing Go programs. In the next chapter, we'll build on this foundation to explore functions and packages, which allow us to structure our code into reusable, modular units.

Chapter 3: Functions and Packages

In the previous chapter, we learned about the basic building blocks of Go programs - variables, types, expressions, and control flow statements. In this chapter, we'll take a step up in abstraction and learn about functions and packages, which allow us to structure our code into reusable, modular units.

Defining and Calling Functions

A function is a block of code that performs a specific task. It takes zero or more parameters as input, does some processing, and optionally returns one or more values. Functions allow us to break our code into smaller, more manageable pieces, and to reuse code without having to copy and paste it.

In Go, a function is defined with the func keyword, followed by the function name, a list of parameters in parentheses, a list of return types, and the function body in curly braces. Here's a simple example:

```go
Copy
func greet(name string) string {
    return "Hello, " + name + "!"
}
```

This function, named greet, takes one parameter of type string (the name of the person to greet), and returns a string (the greeting message).

To call a function, we simply use its name followed by a list of arguments in parentheses:

```go
Copy
message := greet("Alice")
fmt.Println(message)   // Output: Hello, Alice!
```

Functions can have zero or more parameters, and zero or more return values. If a function has multiple return values, they are separated by commas:

```go
Copy
func swap(x, y string) (string, string) {
    return y, x
}

a, b := swap("hello", "world")
fmt.Println(a, b)   // Output: world hello
```

Functions can also have named return values. In this case, the return values are declared as variables at the start of the function, and a bare return statement returns these values:

```go
Copy
func split(sum int) (x, y int) {
    x = sum * 4 / 9
    y = sum - x
    return
}

fmt.Println(split(17))   // Output: 7 10
```

CHAPTER 3: FUNCTIONS AND PACKAGES

Function Parameters and Return Values

Function parameters are the inputs to a function. They are declared within the parentheses in the function declaration, as a list of names and types. For example:

```go
Copy
func add(x int, y int) int {
    return x + y
}
```

Here, x and y are the parameters, both of type int. When calling the function, we provide the arguments in the same order:

```go
Copy
fmt.Println(add(42, 13))   // Output: 55
```

If consecutive parameters have the same type, we can omit the type from all but the last:

```go
Copy
func add(x, y int) int {
    return x + y
}
```

Functions can also take a variable number of arguments, using a parameter of type ...T where T is the type of the arguments:

```go
Copy
func sum(nums ...int) int {
    total := 0
```

```go
    for _, num := range nums {
        total += num
    }
    return total
}

fmt.Println(sum(1, 2, 3))
    // Output: 6
fmt.Println(sum(1, 2, 3, 4))
// Output: 10
```

Here, nums is a slice of int containing all the arguments passed to sum.

As we saw earlier, functions can also return multiple values. This is often used to return a result and an error:

```go
Copy
func divide(x, y float64) (float64, error) {
    if y == 0 {
        return 0, errors.New("division by zero")
    }
    return x / y, nil
}

result, err := divide(5, 2)
if err != nil {
    fmt.Println("Error:", err)
} else {
    fmt.Println("Result:", result)
}
```

Here, divide returns two values: the result of the division, and an error value. If the division is successful, the error will be nil.

CHAPTER 3: FUNCTIONS AND PACKAGES

Anonymous Functions

An anonymous function is a function without a name. These are useful when you want to define a function inline without naming it. Anonymous functions are often used as arguments to other functions, or as immediately invoked function expressions (IIFEs).

Here's an example of an anonymous function being passed as an argument to another function:

```go
Copy
func apply(x, y int, op func(int, int) int) int {
return op(x, y)
}

add := func(x, y int) int {
return x + y
}

fmt.Println(apply(2, 3, add)) // Output: 5
fmt.Println(apply(2, 3, func(x, y int) int {
return x - y
})) // Output: -1
```

In this example, apply is a function that takes two ints and a function op as parameters, and returns the result of calling op with the two ints. We pass an anonymous function to apply in two ways: first by assigning it to a variable add, and second by defining it inline in the call to apply.

Anonymous functions can also be immediately invoked:

```go
Copy
```

```
func() {
    fmt.Println
("Hello from an IIFE!")
}()
```

This defines an anonymous function and immediately calls it.

Packages and Imports

A package is a way to group related functions, types, and variables together. Every Go program is made up of packages. Programs start running in the main package, which is why we've been using package main at the top of our examples.

Here's an example of a simple package (greetings.go):

```go
Copy
package greetings

func Hello(name string) string {
return "Hello, " + name + "!"
}
```

To use this package in another file, we need to import it:

```go
Copy
package main

import (
"fmt"
"example.com/greetings"
)

func main() {
```

```go
    fmt.Println(greetings.
Hello("Alice"))
}
```

Here, we import the greetings package (assuming it's located at example.com/greetings) and use its Hello function in our main function.

The import statement can import multiple packages at once, as shown here. It can also use a shorter alias for a package:

```go
Copy
import g "example.com/greetings"

fmt.Println(g
.Hello("Alice"))
```

When you import a package, you can only refer to its exported names. A name is exported if it begins with a capital letter. In our greetings package, Hello is exported, but if we had a function named hello, it would not be accessible from outside the package.

Creating and Using Custom Packages

Let's walk through creating and using a custom package. We'll create a simple math package with a few basic functions.

First, create a new directory for your package, and a new Go file inside it (math.go):

```go
Copy
package math

func Add(x, y int) int {
    return x + y
```

```go
}

func Subtract(x, y int) int {
    return x - y
}
```

Now, in a separate directory, create a new Go file that imports and uses your math package:

```go
Copy
package main

import (
    "fmt"
    "example.com/math"
)

func main() {
    fmt.Println(math.Add(2, 3))
    // Output: 5
    fmt.Println(math.Subtract(5, 2)) // Output: 3
}
```

To use your custom package, you'll need to set your GOPATH to the parent directory of your package directory, and use the full path to your package in the import statement (example.com/math in this case).

You can also create sub-packages within your package. For example, you could have a geometry package inside your math package:

```
Copy
math/
math.go
geometry/
geometry.go
```

To use this sub-package, you would import example.com/math/geometry.

Creating custom packages is a powerful way to organize and reuse your code. It allows you to encapsulate related functionality, control visibility (through exported/unexported names), and build a library of useful functions and types that you can share across multiple projects.

In the next chapter, we'll dive deeper into one of Go's most powerful features: structs and interfaces, which allow us to define our own types and specify behavior through methods.

Chapter 4: Structs and Interfaces

In the previous chapter, we learned about functions and packages, which allow us to organize our code into reusable, modular units. In this chapter, we'll take a step further and learn about structs and interfaces, which allow us to define our own types and specify behavior.

Defining and Using Structs

A struct is a typed collection of fields. It's used to group data together to form a record. Here's an example of a simple struct:

```go
Copy
type Person struct {
    Name string
    Age  int
}
```

This defines a new type Person which is a struct with two fields: Name of type string and Age of type int.

We can create an instance of our Person struct like this:

```go
Copy
person := Person{"Alice", 30}
```

Or, if we want to name the fields:

```go
Copy
person := Person{Name: "Alice", Age: 30}
```

We can access the fields of a struct using the dot notation:

```go
Copy
fmt.Println(person.Name) // Output: Alice
fmt.Println(person.Age)  // Output: 30
```

Structs are often used to group related data together. For example, if we're writing a program to handle geometric shapes, we might define structs like this:

```go
Copy
type Point struct {
    X, Y float64
}

type Circle struct {
    Center Point
    Radius float64
}

type Rectangle struct {
    TopLeft, BottomRight Point
}
```

Here, we have a Point struct representing a point in 2D space, a Circle struct that contains a Point for the center and a float64 for the radius, and a Rectangle struct that contains two Points for the top-left and bottom-right corners.

We can nest structs within other structs, as we've done with Point inside Circle and Rectangle. This allows us to build complex types out of simpler ones.

Methods and Receivers

A method is a function with a special receiver argument. The receiver appears in its own argument list between the func keyword and the method name. Here's an example:

```go
Copy
func (p Person) SayHello() {
    fmt.Printf("Hello, my name is %s and I am %d years old.\n",
        p.Name, p.Age)
}
```

This defines a method SayHello on the Person struct. The (p Person) before the method name is the receiver, which specifies on what type the method is defined. Inside the method, p is like a variable referring to the Person instance the method is being called on.

We can call this method like this:

```go
Copy
person := Person{"Alice", 30}
person.SayHello() // Output: Hello, my name is Alice and I am 30 years old.
```

Methods can be defined on any type, not just structs. But you can only define a method with a receiver whose type is defined in the same package as the method.

Methods are a powerful tool for abstraction and encapsulation. They allow us to associate behavior with data, and to hide implementation details behind a clean interface.

Let's extend our geometric types with some methods:

```go
Copy
func (p Point) Distance(q Point) float64 {
    return math.Hypot(q.X-p.X, q.Y-p.Y)
}

func (c Circle) Area() float64 {
    return math.Pi * c.Radius * c.Radius
}

func (r Rectangle) Area() float64 {
    return (r.BottomRight.X - r.TopLeft.X) * (r.TopLeft.Y - r.BottomRight.Y)
}
```

Here we've added a Distance method to Point for calculating the distance between two points, and Area methods to Circle and Rectangle for calculating their respective areas.

We can call these methods like this:

```go
Copy
p := Point{1, 2}
q := Point{4, 6}
fmt.Println(p.Distance(q)) // Output: 5

c := Circle{Point{0, 0}, 5}
fmt.Println(c.Area()) // Output: 78.53981633974483

r := Rectangle{Point{0, 0}, Point{10, 10}}
fmt.Println(r.Area()) // Output: 100
```

Methods allow us to write expressive, readable code. Instead of having a separate function for calculating the area of a circle, we can simply call the

Area method on our Circle instance.

Interfaces and Polymorphism

An interface type is defined as a set of method signatures. A value of interface type can hold any value that implements those methods. Here's an example:

```go
Copy
type Shape interface {
    Area() float64
}
```

This defines an interface type Shape, which has a single method Area that takes no arguments and returns a float64.

A type implements an interface by implementing its methods. There is no explicit declaration of intent, no "implements" keyword. Here's an example:

```go
Copy
func (c Circle) Area() float64 {
    return math.Pi * c.Radius * c.Radius
}

func (r Rectangle) Area() float64 {
    return (r.BottomRight.X - r.TopLeft.X) * (r.TopLeft.Y - r.BottomRight.Y)
}
```

Both Circle and Rectangle have an Area method that takes no arguments and returns a float64, so they both implement the Shape interface.

We can use interface types as function parameters:

```go
Copy
```

```go
func PrintArea(s Shape) {
    fmt.Printf("The area is: %f\n", s.Area())
}
```

This function takes a Shape as a parameter, which means it can take any value that implements the Shape interface - a Circle, a Rectangle, or any other type that has an Area method with the right signature.

We can call this function with a Circle or a Rectangle:

```go
Copy
c := Circle{Point{0, 0}, 5}
r := Rectangle{Point{0, 0}, Point{10, 10}}

PrintArea(c) // Output: The area is: 78.539816
PrintArea(r) // Output: The area is: 100.000000
```

This is an example of polymorphism - the ability to treat values of different types uniformly as long as they implement a common interface. The PrintArea function doesn't need to know the specific type of the Shape it's dealing with, it just needs to know that it has an Area method.

Interfaces are a powerful tool for abstraction and decoupling. They allow us to write code that is more flexible and easier to change, because we can depend on interfaces instead of concrete types.

Type Assertions and Type Switches

A type assertion provides access to an interface value's underlying concrete value. Here's the syntax:

```go
Copy
t := i.(T)
```

This statement asserts that the interface value i holds the concrete type T and assigns the underlying T value to the variable t.

If i does not hold a T, the statement will trigger a panic. To avoid this, you can use the "comma, ok" idiom:

```go
Copy
t, ok := i.(T)
```

If i holds a T, then t will be the underlying value and ok will be true. If not, ok will be false and t will be the zero value of type T, and no panic occurs.

Here's an example:

```go
Copy
var i interface{} = "hello"

s := i.(string)
fmt.Println(s) // Output: hello

f, ok := i.(float64)
fmt.Println(f, ok) // Output: 0 false
```

A type switch is a construct that permits several type assertions in series. Here's an example:

```go
Copy
switch v := i.(type) {
case int:
    fmt.Printf("Twice %v is %v\n", v, v*2)
case string:
    fmt.Printf("%q is %v bytes long\n", v, len(v))
default:
    fmt.Printf("I don't know about type %T!\n", v)
}
```

CHAPTER 4: STRUCTS AND INTERFACES

This switch statement on i.(type) asserts the concrete type of the interface value i. In each case, the variable v will be of the type asserted in that branch.

Type assertions and type switches are useful when we need to treat an interface value differently based on its underlying concrete type.

For example, let's say we have a function that takes a Shape and wants to print different things based on whether it's a Circle or a Rectangle:

```go
Copy
func PrintDetails(s Shape) {
    switch v := s.(type) {
    case Circle:
        fmt.Printf("Circle with center at %v and radius %f\n",
            v.Center, v.Radius)
    case Rectangle:
        fmt.Printf("Rectangle with corners at %v and %v\n",
            v.TopLeft, v.BottomRight)
    default:
        fmt.Printf("Unknown shape: %T\n", v)
    }
}
```

This function uses a type switch to access the underlying Circle or Rectangle value of the Shape interface.

Structs and interfaces are two of the most powerful features of Go. They allow us to create well-organized, modular code that is easy to understand, test, and maintain. By defining our own types and specifying their behavior through methods and interfaces, we can create abstractions that make our code more expressive and flexible.

In the next section, we'll put all of our knowledge together and start building real-world applications in Go.

Section II: Building Real-World Applications Chapter 5: Command-Line Tools

In the first section of this book, we covered the fundamentals of the Go programming language. We learned about variables, types, functions, packages, structs, and interfaces - the building blocks of any Go program.

In this section, we'll put that knowledge to use and start building real-world applications in Go. We'll cover a variety of practical topics and work through several hands-on projects that will help solidify your understanding of Go and give you experience with the tools and techniques used in real-world Go development.

Chapter 5: Command-Line Tools

Command-line tools, also known as CLI (Command-Line Interface) tools, are programs that are run from a terminal or command prompt. They take input in the form of arguments and flags, perform some operation, and usually print output to the console.

Go is an excellent language for building CLI tools. Its fast compilation, static typing, and easy cross-platform compilation make it ideal for writing tools that need to be portable, reliable, and efficient.

In this chapter, we'll learn how to create CLI tools in Go. We'll cover reading command-line arguments, parsing flags, working with files and directories, and executing system commands. We'll also work through a practical project of building a file search utility.

Reading Command-Line Arguments

When you run a program from the command line, you can pass arguments to it. These arguments are available to your Go program as a slice of strings in the os.Args variable.

Here's a simple example that prints out its command-line arguments:

```go
Copy
package main

import (
    "fmt"
    "os"
)

func main() {
    fmt.Println(os.Args)
}
```

If you save this to a file args.go and run it with some arguments:

```
Copy
go run args.go these are my arguments
```

You'll see output like this:

```
Copy
[/var/folders/temporary_path/go-build2347823289/b001/exe/args
```

these are my arguments]

The first element of os.Args is always the path to the program itself. The rest of the elements are the arguments that were passed to the program.

You can access individual arguments like this:

```go
Copy
func main() {
    if len(os.Args) > 1 {
        fmt.Println("The first argument is:", os.Args[1])
    }
}
```

This checks if at least one argument was passed (remember, the program name itself is always the first element), and if so, prints the first argument.

Parsing Flags

While os.Args gives you access to the raw command-line arguments, it's often more convenient to use flags. Flags allow you to define named options for your program and easily parse them from the command line.

Go's flag package provides support for parsing command-line flags.

Here's an example:

```go
Copy
package main

import (
    "flag"
    "fmt"
)

func main() {
```

```go
    wordPtr := flag.String("word", "foo", "a string")
    numbPtr := flag.Int("numb", 42, "an int")
    boolPtr := flag.Bool("fork", false, "a bool")

    flag.Parse()

    fmt.Println("word:", *wordPtr)
    fmt.Println("numb:", *numbPtr)
    fmt.Println("fork:", *boolPtr)
    fmt.Println("tail:", flag.Args())
}
```

In this example, we define three flags: word (a string flag), numb (an integer flag), and fork (a boolean flag). Each flag is defined with a default value and a help message.

After defining the flags, we call flag.Parse() to parse the command-line arguments. This will assign the parsed values to the variables pointed at by the flags.

Note that the flag variables are pointers. This is because the flag functions need to be able to modify the variables directly. To get the value of a flag, we need to dereference the pointer.

After parsing the flags, any remaining arguments can be accessed with flag.Args().

If you run this program with some flags and arguments:

Copy
```
go run flags.go -word=bar -numb=7 arg1 arg2
```

You'll see output like this:

Copy
```
word: bar
numb: 7
fork: false
tail: [arg1 arg2]
```

The flag package also automatically generates help text for your program. If you run the program with -h or —help, you'll see the automatically generated help text:

```
Copy
go run flags.go --help
```

This will output:

```
Copy
Usage of flags:
  -fork
        a bool
  -numb int
        an int (default 42)
  -word string
        a string (default "foo")
```

Using flags makes your CLI tools more user-friendly and easier to use.

Working with Files and Directories

Many CLI tools need to interact with the file system - reading files, writing files, walking directory trees, etc.

Go's os package provides many functions for working with files and directories.

Here are some examples:

```go
Copy
// Reading a file
data, err := os.ReadFile("file.txt")
if err != nil {
    log.Fatal(err)
```

```go
}
fmt.Println(string(data))

// Writing a file
err := os.WriteFile("file.txt", []byte("Hello, World!"), 0644)
if err != nil {
    log.Fatal(err)
}

// Checking if a file exists
_, err := os.Stat("file.txt")
if os.IsNotExist(err) {
    fmt.Println("File does not exist")
} else {
    fmt.Println("File exists")
}

// Walking a directory tree
err := filepath.Walk(".", func(path string, info os.FileInfo, err error) error {
    if err != nil {
        return err
    }
    fmt.Println(path, info.Size())
    return nil
})
if err != nil {
    log.Fatal(err)
}
```

These are just a few examples. The os and io packages provide many more functions for working with files and directories.

Executing System Commands

Sometimes your CLI tool might need to execute other programs. Go makes this easy with the os/exec package.

Here's an example of running a command and capturing its output:

```go
Copy
cmd := exec.Command("echo", "Hello, World!")
stdout, err := cmd.Output()
if err != nil {
    log.Fatal(err)
}
fmt.Println(string(stdout))
```

This uses exec.Command to create a command (echo with the argument "Hello, World!"), then runs the command and captures its output with cmd.Output().

You can also use cmd.Run() to run a command and wait for it to finish, or cmd.Start() to start a command and continue executing your Go program concurrently.

The os/exec package provides more advanced features like setting environment variables, specifying the working directory, and connecting to the command's standard input, output, and error streams.

Project: Building a File Search Utility

Now let's put our knowledge to use and build a practical CLI tool in Go. We'll create a tool that searches for files in a directory tree that match a given pattern.

Here's the code:

```go
Copy
package main

import (
    "flag"
    "fmt"
```

```go
    "log"
    "os"
    "path/filepath"
    "regexp"
)

func main() {
    // Define command-line flags
    pattern := flag.String("pattern", "", "Search pattern (regular expression)")
    directory := flag.String("directory", ".", "Directory to search")
    recursive := flag.Bool("recursive", false, "Search recursively")

    // Parse flags
    flag.Parse()

    // Compile the regular expression
    regex, err := regexp.Compile(*pattern)
    if err != nil {
        log.Fatal(err)
    }

    // Walk the directory tree
    err = filepath.Walk(*directory, func(path string, info os.FileInfo, err error) error {
        if err != nil {
            return err
        }

        // If the file matches the pattern, print its path
        if regex.MatchString(info.Name()) {
            fmt.Println(path)
        }

        // If recursive is false and we're in a directory other
        // than the starting one, skip it
        if !*recursive && info.IsDir() && path != *directory {
            return filepath.SkipDir
```

```
        }

        return nil
    })

    if err != nil {
        log.Fatal(err)
    }
}
```

Let's break this down:

1. We define three command-line flags: pattern (the search pattern, a regular expression), directory (the directory to search, defaults to the current directory), and recursive (whether to search recursively, defaults to false).
2. We parse the flags with flag.Parse().
3. We compile the regular expression with regexp.Compile. This allows us to use the same regular expression for multiple searches and improves performance.
4. We use filepath.Walk to walk the directory tree. For each file:

- If the file name matches the search pattern (checked with regex.MatchString), we print its path.
- If recursive is false and we're in a directory other than the starting directory, we skip that directory with filepath.SkipDir. This makes the search non-recursive.

1. If any error occurs during the walk, we log it and exit.

You can build this program with:

```
Copy
go build search.go
```

And then run it with various flags:

```
Copy
./search -pattern='\\.go$' -directory=/path/to/project -recursive
```

This will search recursively in /path/to/project for all files ending with .go.

This is a simple but useful tool that demonstrates many of the concepts we've covered in this chapter - command-line flags, file system operations, and executing code based on user input.

Of course, this is just a starting point. You could extend this tool in many ways - allowing multiple search patterns, enabling case-insensitive searches, printing line numbers for matches within files, etc. The possibilities are endless!

Building CLI tools is a great way to automate tasks, improve your workflow, and share useful utilities with others. With Go's powerful standard library and easy cross-platform compilation, it's a fantastic language for creating CLI tools.

In the next chapter, we'll dive into another exciting area of Go development - web applications. We'll learn how to build web servers, handle HTTP requests, serve static files, and create dynamic HTML templates. Get ready to take your Go skills to the web!

Chapter 7: Concurrent Programming

One of the standout features of Go is its built-in support for concurrent programming. Go makes it easy to write programs that can effectively utilize modern multi-core CPUs and handle concurrent operations elegantly.

In this chapter, we'll explore Go's concurrency primitives and learn how to use them to write concurrent programs. We'll cover goroutines, channels, synchronization with the sync package, common concurrency patterns, and the context package for managing cancellation and deadlines. Finally, we'll put our knowledge into practice by building a concurrent web scraper.

Goroutines and Channels

The foundation of Go's concurrency model is goroutines and channels.

Goroutines

A goroutine is a lightweight thread managed by the Go runtime. Goroutines are incredibly cheap to create and manage, and a single program can have thousands or even millions of goroutines running concurrently.

You start a new goroutine by calling a function prefixed with the go keyword. Here's a simple example:

```go
Copy
func main() {
go sayHello()
// do other work...
time.Sleep(100 * time.Millisecond)
}

func sayHello() {
fmt.Println("Hello")
}
```

In this example, sayHello is called as a goroutine. The main function continues to execute concurrently with sayHello. We add a small sleep at the end of main to give the sayHello goroutine a chance to run before the program exits.

Channels

Channels provide a way for goroutines to communicate and synchronize with each other. A channel is a typed conduit through which you can send and receive values with the channel operator, <-.

Here's an example:

```go
Copy
func main() {
ch := make(chan string)
go sayHello(ch)
msg := <-ch
fmt.Println(msg)
}

func sayHello(ch chan string) {
ch <- "Hello"
}
```

In this example, we create a channel of strings with make(chan string). We pass this channel to the sayHello goroutine. Inside sayHello, we send the string "Hello" to the channel with ch <- "Hello". Back in main, we receive from the channel with msg := <-ch, which blocks until a value is available.

Channels can be buffered or unbuffered. An unbuffered channel blocks the sender until the receiver is ready to receive the value. A buffered channel has a buffer of a specified size, and sends to the channel block only when the buffer is full.

Here's how you create a buffered channel with a buffer size of 10:

```go
Copy
ch := make(chan int, 10)
```

Channels are a powerful tool for coordinating goroutines and implementing various concurrency patterns, which we'll explore later in this chapter.

Synchronization with sync Package

In concurrent programming, it's often necessary to synchronize access to shared resources to avoid race conditions. Go's standard library provides the sync package for this purpose.

Mutexes

A mutex (mutual exclusion lock) is a synchronization primitive that allows at most one goroutine to access a shared resource at a time. The sync.Mutex type represents a mutex in Go.

Here's an example of using a mutex to synchronize access to a shared variable:

```go
Copy
```

```go
var count int
var mutex sync.Mutex

func increment() {
    mutex.Lock()
    count++
    mutex.Unlock()
}

func main() {
    for i := 0; i < 1000; i++ {
    go increment()
        }
    time.Sleep(100 * time.Millisecond)
    fmt.Println("Count:", count)
}
```

In this example, we have a shared count variable that is incremented by multiple goroutines. To avoid race conditions, we use a sync.Mutex to ensure that only one goroutine can access count at a time. Before accessing count, a goroutine must acquire the lock with mutex.Lock(), and after it's done, it releases the lock with mutex.Unlock().

WaitGroups

Another common synchronization need is to wait for a group of goroutines to finish before proceeding. The sync.WaitGroup type provides this functionality.

Here's an example:

```go
Copy
var wg sync.WaitGroup

func worker(id int) {
    defer wg.Done()
```

```go
    fmt.Printf("Worker
%d starting\n", id)
    time.Sleep(time.Second)
    fmt.Printf("Worker
 %d done\n", id)
}

func main() {
    for i := 1; i
  <= 5; i++ {
wg.Add(1)
go worker(i)
    }
wg.Wait()
}
```

In this example, we start 5 worker goroutines. Before starting each goroutine, we increment the WaitGroup counter with wg.Add(1). Each worker signals that it's done by calling wg.Done(), which decrements the counter. In main, we wait for all workers to finish with wg.Wait(), which blocks until the counter reaches zero.

Patterns for Concurrency

There are several common patterns in Go for structuring concurrent programs. Let's look at a few of them.

Generator Pattern

The generator pattern involves a function that returns a channel, which it writes data to. The channel is then consumed by the caller.

Here's an example of a generator that produces a sequence of numbers:

```
go
Copy
```

CHAPTER 7: CONCURRENT PROGRAMMING

```go
func generator(n int) <-chan int {
out := make(chan int)
go func() {
for i := 0; i < n; i++ {
out <- i
        }
close(out)
    }()
return out
}

func main() {
for i := range generator(10) {
fmt.Println(i)
    }
}
```

In this example, the generator function creates a channel, starts a goroutine that writes numbers to the channel, and returns the channel. The main function consumes the numbers from the channel using a for range loop.

Fan-Out, Fan-In Pattern

The fan-out, fan-in pattern involves starting multiple goroutines to handle input, and then combining their results into a single channel.

Here's an example that squares numbers in parallel:

```go
Copy
func square(in <-chan int) <-chan int {
out := make(chan int)
go func() {
for n := range in {
out <- n * n
        }
close(out)
    }()
```

55

```go
	return out
}

func merge(cs ...<-chan int) <-chan int {
	var wg sync.WaitGroup
	out := make(chan int)

	output := func(c <-chan int) {
		for n := range c {
			out <- n
		}
		wg.Done()
	}

	wg.Add(len(cs))
	for _, c := range cs {
		go output(c)
	}

	go func() {
		wg.Wait()
		close(out)
	}()
	return out
}

func main() {
	in := generator(100)

	c1 := square(in)
	c2 := square(in)
	c3 := square(in)

	for n := range merge(c1, c2, c3) {
		fmt.Println(n)
	}
}
```

In this example, the square function reads numbers from an input channel, squares them, and writes the results to an output channel. We create three instances of square, each reading from the same input channel (fan-out). The merge function reads from multiple channels and writes all the values to a single output channel (fan-in).

Select

The select statement in Go is used to choose from multiple send/receive channel operations. It blocks until one of the cases can proceed, then it executes that case. It chooses one at random if multiple are ready.

Here's an example of using select to implement a timeout:

```go
Copy
func main() {
c1 := make(chan string)
go func() {
time.Sleep(2 * time.Second)
c1 <- "result 1"
    }()

select {
case res := <-c1:
fmt.Println(res)
case <-time.After(1 * time.Second):
fmt.Println("timeout 1")
    }
}
```

In this example, we start a goroutine that sends a value on c1 after 2 seconds. The select statement waits either for a value to be received from c1, or for a timeout of 1 second. Since the timeout is shorter, the select will proceed with the timeout case.

The Context Package

The context package in Go provides a way to manage cancellation, deadlines, and request-scoped values across API boundaries and goroutines.

A Context is created with context.Background() or context.TODO() and then derived from using context.WithCancel, context.WithDeadline, or context.WithTimeout.

Here's an example of using context for cancellation:

```go
Copy
func worker(ctx context.
Context, wg *sync.
WaitGroup) error {
    defer wg.Done()

    for {
select {
default:
fmt.Println("working...")
time.Sleep(time.Second)
case <-ctx.Done():
return ctx.Err()
        }
    }
}

func main() {
ctx, cancel := context.WithTimeout
(context.Background(),
 5*time.Second)
defer cancel()
var wg sync.WaitGroup
wg.Add(1)
go worker(ctx, &wg)

    wg.Wait()
}
```

In this example, we create a context with a timeout of 5 seconds using context.WithTimeout. We pass this context to the worker goroutine. The worker does its work in a loop, but it checks the context's Done channel on each iteration. When the context's deadline expires, the worker returns.

The context package is a powerful tool for managing concurrency across goroutine and API boundaries, especially in larger applications with complex concurrency requirements.

Project: Concurrent Web Scraper

Now let's put our concurrency knowledge into practice by building a concurrent web scraper. Our scraper will take a list of URLs, fetch the content of each URL concurrently, and record some basic statistics about each page.

Here's the code:

```go
Copy
type result struct {
    url     string
    size    int
    words   int
}

func main() {
urls := []string{
"https://www.golang.org/",
"https://www.google.com/",
"https://www.bbc.com/",
    }

results := make(chan result)

for _, url := range urls {
go func(url string) {
res, err := http.Get(url)
```

```go
if err != nil {
log.Fatal(err)
            }
defer res.Body.Close()

body, err := ioutil.ReadAll(res.Body)
if err != nil {
log.Fatal(err)
                }

words := strings.Fields(string(body))

results <- result{url, len(body), len(words)}
}(url)
    }

var total int
for range urls {
res := <-results
fmt.Printf("Count for %s: %d bytes, %d words\n", res.url, res.size, res.words)
total += res.size
    }
fmt.Printf("Total size: %d bytes\n", total)
}
```

In this code:

1. We define a result struct to hold the URL, size, and word count of each page.
2. We create a channel results to receive the results of each scrape.
3. For each URL, we start a goroutine that fetches the page, counts the bytes and words, and sends a result struct to the results channel.
4. In the main goroutine, we range over the URLs, receiving each result

CHAPTER 7: CONCURRENT PROGRAMMING

from the results channel and printing it. We also keep a running total of the bytes scraped.
5. Finally, we print the total bytes scraped.

This simple program demonstrates the power of Go's concurrency primitives. Each page is fetched concurrently, allowing the program to efficiently scrape multiple pages. The main goroutine waits for each result and aggregates the results.

Of course, this is just a starting point. You could extend this scraper to follow links, handle errors more gracefully, respect rate limits, and much more. But the basic structure - using goroutines for concurrent work and channels for communication - will remain the same.

Concurrency is a vast and complex topic, and this chapter has only scratched the surface. But with an understanding of goroutines, channels, the sync and context packages, and common concurrency patterns, you're well-equipped to start writing efficient, concurrent Go programs.

In the next chapter, we'll explore another crucial aspect of real-world programming: interacting with databases. We'll learn how to use Go's database/sql package to query and update SQL databases, and we'll build a simple CRUD (Create, Read, Update, Delete) application. Get ready to level up your Go skills even further!

Chapter 8: Working with Databases

Most real-world applications need to persist data, and databases are the most common way to do this. Whether you're building a simple todo list application or a complex e-commerce platform, you'll likely need to interact with a database.

Go has excellent support for working with databases. Its database/sql package provides a generic interface for SQL (or SQL-like) databases, and there are many third-party drivers available for popular databases like MySQL, PostgreSQL, and SQLite.

In this chapter, we'll learn how to use Go to interact with SQL databases. We'll cover connecting to databases, executing queries and statements, mapping database data to Go structs, and managing database schemas with migrations. Finally, we'll put everything together by building a simple CRUD (Create, Read, Update, Delete) API.

Connecting to SQL Databases

The first step in working with a database is establishing a connection. In Go, this is done using the database/sql package and a database-specific driver.

Here's an example of connecting to a MySQL database:

CHAPTER 8: WORKING WITH DATABASES

```go
Copy
import (
"database/sql"
_ "github.com/
go-sql-driver/mysql"
)

func main() {
db, err := sql.Open
("mysql", "user:password@tcp
(127.0.0.1:3306)/database")
if err != nil {
log.Fatal(err)
    }
defer db.Close()
}
```

In this code:

1. We import the database/sql package and the MySQL driver. The _ before the driver import means we want the side effect of the driver registering itself with database/sql, but we don't directly reference the package in our code.
2. We use sql.Open to create a new sql.DB instance. The first argument is the driver name, and the second is the data source name (DSN), which includes the username, password, host, port, and database name.
3. We defer the closing of the database connection until the surrounding function returns.

The process is similar for other databases, but the DSN format may be different. For example, here's how you might connect to a PostgreSQL database:

```go
Copy
db, err := sql.Open("postgres",
"user=username
 password=password host=
localhost port=5432
dbname=mydb sslmode=disable")
```

And here's an example for SQLite, which uses a file as its data store:

```go
Copy
db, err := sql.Open
("sqlite3",
"path/to/database.db")
```

It's important to note that sql.Open doesn't actually establish any connections to the database. It simply prepares the database abstraction for later use. The actual connections are established lazily, as needed.

Executing Queries and Statements

Once you have a database connection, you can use it to execute SQL queries and statements. The database/sql package provides several methods for this.

Queries

To execute a query that returns rows, you can use the DB.Query method:

```go
Copy
rows, err := db.Query
("SELECT id, name FROM users
 WHERE age > ?", 18)
if err != nil {
```

CHAPTER 8: WORKING WITH DATABASES

```go
        log.Fatal(err)
    }
    defer rows.Close()

    for rows.Next() {
        var (
            id   int
            name string
        )
        err := rows.Scan(&id, &name)
        if err != nil {
            log.Fatal(err)
        }
        fmt.Printf("id: %d, name: %s\n", id, name)
    }

    err = rows.Err()
    if err != nil {
        log.Fatal(err)
    }
```

In this code:

1. We use DB.Query to execute a SELECT query. The ? in the query is a placeholder for a parameter, which is provided as an additional argument.
2. We defer the closing of the rows until the surrounding function returns.
3. We iterate over the rows using rows.Next(). This prepares the next row for reading with rows.Scan.
4. Inside the loop, we define variables to hold the values of the columns we're interested in. We use rows.Scan to assign the columns to these variables.
5. After the loop, we check for any errors that occurred during iteration with rows.Err().

If you're expecting a single row, you can use DB.QueryRow instead:

```go
Copy
var (
    id   int
    name string
)
err := db.QueryRow
("SELECT id, name FROM
 users WHERE id = ?", 1).
Scan(&id, &name)
if err != nil {
if err == sql.ErrNoRows {
// no rows found
} else {
log.Fatal(err)
    }
}
fmt.Printf("id: %d,
name: %s\n", id, name)
```

DB.QueryRow returns a single row. You can call Scan directly on the result to assign the columns to variables. If no rows are found, Scan will return sql.ErrNoRows.

Statements

For SQL statements that don't return rows (like INSERT, UPDATE, and DELETE), you can use DB.Exec:

```go
Copy
result, err := db.
Exec("INSERT INTO users
(name, age) VALUES
(?, ?)", "Alice", 30)
```

```go
if err != nil {
    log.Fatal(err)
}

lastId, err := result.LastInsertId()
if err != nil {
    log.Fatal(err)
}
fmt.Printf("Inserted row with ID: %d\n", lastId)

rowsAffected, err := result.RowsAffected()
if err != nil {
    log.Fatal(err)
}
fmt.Printf("Inserted %d row(s)\n", rowsAffected)
```

DB.Exec returns a sql.Result, which provides methods for retrieving the last inserted ID (LastInsertId) and the number of rows affected (RowsAffected).

Prepared Statements

If you're executing the same query or statement multiple times with different parameters, you can use a prepared statement for better efficiency and security:

```go
Copy
stmt, err := db.Prepare
("SELECT id, name
FROM users WHERE age > ?")
if err != nil {
    log.Fatal(err)
```

```
}
defer stmt.Close()

rows, err := stmt.Query(18)
if err != nil {
log.Fatal(err)
}
defer rows.Close()

for rows.Next() {
    // ...
}
```

You create a prepared statement with DB.Prepare, and then execute it multiple times with different arguments using Stmt.Query or Stmt.Exec.

Mapping Data to Structs

In the previous examples, we manually assigned columns to individual variables. This can be tedious and error-prone, especially for structs with many fields.

Fortunately, Go provides a way to automatically map columns to struct fields. You can do this by defining a struct with db tags:

```go
Copy
type User struct {
ID      int     `db:"id"`
Name    string  `db:"name"`
Age     int     `db:"age"`
}
```

The db tag tells the SQL package which column each field corresponds to.

You can then use this struct with DB.QueryRow or DB.Query and rows.Scan:

CHAPTER 8: WORKING WITH DATABASES

```go
var user User
err := db.QueryRow
("SELECT id, name, age
FROM users WHERE id = ?", 1).
Scan(&user.ID, &user.Name, &user.Age)
if err != nil {
    log.Fatal(err)
}
fmt.Printf("User: %+v\n", user)
```

```go
rows, err := db.Query
("SELECT id, name, age FROM users")
if err != nil {
    log.Fatal(err)
}
defer rows.Close()

var users []User
for rows.Next() {
var user User
err := rows.Scan
(&user.ID, &user.
Name, &user.Age)
if err != nil {
log.Fatal(err)
    }
users = append(users, user)
}
fmt.Printf("Users: %+v\n", users)
```

This makes the code much cleaner and less error-prone.

Database Migrations

Over the life of an application, the structure of its database will likely change. Tables will be added, removed, or altered. These changes need to be managed carefully, especially in production environments.

Database migrations are a way to manage these changes. Migrations are a sequence of SQL scripts that modify the database schema, organized in a way that allows them to be applied and rolled back in a predictable order.

There are several libraries in Go for managing database migrations. One popular one is golang-migrate/migrate. Here's an example of how to use it:

```go
Copy
import (
    "database/sql"
    _ "github.com/go-sql-driver/mysql"
    "github.com/golang-migrate/migrate/v4"
    _ "github.com/golang-migrate/migrate/v4/database/mysql"
    _ "github.com/golang-migrate/migrate/v4/source/file"
)

func main() {
    db, err := sql.Open("mysql", "user:password@tcp(127.0.0.1:3306)/database")
    if err != nil {
        log.Fatal(err)
    }
    defer db.Close()

    m, err := migrate.New(
```

CHAPTER 8: WORKING WITH DATABASES

```
"file://path/to/migration/files",
"mysql://user:password
@tcp(127.0.0.1:3306)/database")
if err != nil {
log.Fatal(err)
    }

if err := m.Up(); err != nil {
log.Fatal(err)
    }
}
```

In this code:

1. We import the necessary packages. Note that we need the MySQL driver for both database/sql and golang-migrate/migrate.
2. We create a sql.DB instance as usual.
3. We create a new migrate.Migrate instance, specifying the location of our migration files and the URL of our database.
4. We apply all pending migrations with m.Up(). This will apply migrations in the correct order until the database is up to date.

Migration files are usually organized in pairs: one file for "up" (applying the change) and one for "down" (rolling back the change). Here's an example of an "up" file that creates a users table:

```sql
Copy
CREATE TABLE IF NOT EXISTS users (
id INT AUTO_INCREMENT PRIMARY KEY,
name VARCHAR(255) NOT NULL,
age INT NOT NULL
);
```

And here's the corresponding "down" file:

```sql
Copy
DROP TABLE IF EXISTS users;
```

With golang-migrate/migrate, these files would be named something like 000001_create_users_table.up.sql and 000001_create_users_table.down.sql.

Using migrations ensures that your database schema is versioned and can be safely evolved over time.

Project: Building a CRUD API

Now let's put everything we've learned together into a practical project. We'll build a simple REST API for managing "products". Our API will allow clients to create, read, update, and delete products.

Here's the code for our API:

```go
Copy
package main

import (
"database/sql"
"encoding/json"
"fmt"
"log"
"net/http"
"strconv"

_ "github.com/go-sql-driver/mysql"
"github.com/gorilla/mux"
)

type Product struct {
ID      int
`json:"id"`
Name    string
```

CHAPTER 8: WORKING WITH DATABASES

```go
`json:"name"`
Price float64
 `json:"price"`
}

func main() {
db, err := sql.Open("mysql",
 "user:password@tcp
(127.0.0.1:3306)/database")
if err != nil {
log.Fatal(err)
    }
defer db.Close()

r := mux.NewRouter()

r.HandleFunc("/products",
 createProduct(db)).
Methods("POST")
r.HandleFunc("/products", getProducts(db)).Methods("GET")
r.HandleFunc("/products/{id}", getProduct(db)).Methods("GET")
r.HandleFunc("/products/{id}", updateProduct(db)).Methods("PUT")
r.HandleFunc("/products/{id}",
 deleteProduct(db)).
Methods("DELETE")

log.Fatal(http.
ListenAndServe(":8000", r))
}

func createProduct(db *sql.DB)
 http.HandlerFunc {
return func
(w http.ResponseWriter,
 r *http.Request) {
var p Product
json.NewDecoder
(r.Body).Decode(&p)
result, err := db.Exec
("INSERT INTO products
```

```go
(name, price) VALUES
(?, ?)", p.Name, p.Price)
if err != nil {
log.Fatal(err)
        }

id, err := result.
LastInsertId()
if err != nil {
log.Fatal(err)
        }

p.ID = int(id)

json.NewEncoder(w).Encode(p)
    }
}

func getProducts(db *sql.DB)
 http.HandlerFunc {
return func(w http.
ResponseWriter, r *http.Request) {
rows, err := db.Query
("SELECT id, name,
 price FROM products")
if err != nil {
log.Fatal(err)
        }
defer rows.Close()

var products []Product

for rows.Next() {
var p Product
err := rows.Scan(&p.ID,
&p.Name, &p.Price)
if err != nil {
log.Fatal(err)
            }
products = append(products, p)
```

```go
        }

json.NewEncoder(w).
Encode(products)
    }
}

func getProduct(db *sql.DB)
 http.HandlerFunc {
return func(w http.
ResponseWriter,
r *http.Request) {
params := mux.Vars(r)
id, err := strconv.Atoi(params["id"])
if err != nil {
log.Fatal(err)
        }

var p Product
err = db.QueryRow
("SELECT id, name,
 price FROM products WHERE id =
?", id).Scan(&p.ID,
&p.Name, &p.Price)
if err != nil {
if err == sql.ErrNoRows {
http.NotFound(w, r)
return
        }
log.Fatal(err)
        }

json.NewEncoder(w).Encode(p)
    }
}

func updateProduct(db *sql.DB)
 http.HandlerFunc {
return func(w http.
ResponseWriter, r *http.Request) {
```

```go
params := mux.Vars(r)
id, err := strconv.Atoi(params["id"])
if err != nil {
log.Fatal(err)
        }

var p Product
json.NewDecoder(r.Body).
Decode(&p)
p.ID = id

_, err = db.Exec
("UPDATE products SET name = ?,
price = ? WHERE id = ?",
 p.Name, p.Price, p.ID)
if err != nil {
log.Fatal(err)
        }

json.NewEncoder(w).Encode(p)
    }
}

func deleteProduct(db *sql.DB)
http.HandlerFunc {
return func(w http.ResponseWriter,
r *http.Request) {
params := mux.Vars(r)
id, err := strconv.Atoi(params["id"])
if err != nil {
log.Fatal(err)
        }

_, err = db.Exec(
"DELETE FROM products
 WHERE id = ?", id)
if err != nil {
log.Fatal(err)
        }
```

CHAPTER 8: WORKING WITH DATABASES

```
w.WriteHeader(http.StatusNoContent)
    }
}
```

In this code:

1. We define a Product struct to represent a product in our system. We use json tags to control how the struct is serialized to and from JSON.
2. In our main function, we establish a connection to our MySQL database and create a new mux router.
3. We define routes for each of our CRUD operations, mapping them to the appropriate HTTP methods and handler functions.
4. Each handler function is defined separately. They all follow a similar pattern:

- They accept a *sql.DB and return an http.HandlerFunc.
- They perform the necessary database operation using DB.Exec, DB.Query, or DB.QueryRow.
- They encode the result as JSON and write it to the http.ResponseWriter.

Section III: Leveling Up Your Go Skills
Chapter 9: Testing and Benchmarking

In the previous section, we learned how to build real-world applications in Go. We covered topics like command-line tools, web applications, concurrent programming, and interacting with databases.

In this section, we'll take our Go skills to the next level. We'll cover topics that are essential for writing high-quality, maintainable, and performant Go code. We'll start with testing and benchmarking, then move on to debugging, error handling, and advanced language features.

Chapter 9: Testing and Benchmarking

Testing is an essential part of writing reliable software. It helps ensure that your code works as expected, and it gives you confidence to refactor and extend your code without breaking existing functionality.

Go has excellent built-in support for testing and benchmarking. In this chapter, we'll learn how to write and run tests using the testing package, how to structure your code to be testable, how to use test fixtures and helper functions, and how to benchmark and profile your code.

SECTION III: LEVELING UP YOUR GO SKILLS ...

Unit Testing with the testing Package

Go's testing package provides support for automated testing of Go packages. It is intended to be used in concert with the go test command.

Here's a simple example of a function and a corresponding test:

```go
Copy
// math.go
package math

func Add(a, b int) int {
return a + b
}
```

```go
Copy
// math_test.go
package math

import "testing"

func TestAdd(t *testing.T) {
got := Add(2, 3)
want := 5
if got != want {
t.Errorf("Add(2, 3) =
  %d; want %d", got, want)
    }
}
```

In this example, we have a simple Add function in the math package. In the math_test.go file, we define a test function TestAdd. Test functions always take a single argument of type *testing.T, which provides methods for reporting test failures and logging additional information.

In the test function, we call Add(2, 3) and store the result in got. We then compare got to the expected value want. If they are not equal, we report an error using t.Errorf.

To run the test, we use the go test command:

```
Copy
$ go test
PASS
ok      example/math
    0.001s
```

If the test passes, go test prints "PASS". If the test fails, it prints "FAIL" along with the failure messages.

Table-Driven Tests

In the previous example, we wrote a single test case. However, it's common to want to test a function with multiple inputs and expected outputs. We can do this using a table-driven test:

```go
Copy
func TestAdd(t *testing.T) {
cases := []struct {
a, b int
want int
    }{
{2, 3, 5},
{0, 0, 0},
{-1, 1, 0},
    }
for _, c := range cases {
got := Add(c.a, c.b)
if got != c.want {
t.Errorf("Add(%d, %d)
 == %d, want %d",
 c.a, c.b, got, c.want)
        }
    }
}
```

In this example, we define a slice of anonymous structs, each representing a test case. Each struct has fields for the inputs (a and b) and the expected output (want).

We then iterate over the cases, calling Add with the inputs and comparing the result to the expected output. This makes it easy to add new test cases without duplicating code.

Testing for Errors

It's also important to test that your functions return errors when they should. Here's an example of a function that returns an error and a test that checks for it:

```go
Copy
// divide.go
func Divide(a, b int) (int, error) {
    if b == 0 {
        return 0, errors.New("division by zero")
    }
    return a / b, nil
}
```

```go
Copy
// divide_test.go
func TestDivide(t *testing.T) {
    _, err := Divide(10, 0)
    if err == nil {
        t.Error("Divide (10, 0) should return an error")
    }
}
```

In this example, Divide returns an error when b is zero. The test calls Divide(10, 0) and checks that the error is not nil. If it is nil, the test reports an error.

Writing Testable Code

To write testable code, you need to keep a few principles in mind:

1. Write small, focused functions. Smaller functions are easier to test because they have fewer possible inputs and outputs.
2. Avoid side effects where possible. Functions that modify global state or perform I/O are harder to test because they depend on external factors. Where possible, separate side effects from core logic.
3. Use interfaces to abstract dependencies. If your code depends on an external service or a complex type, define an interface for that dependency. In your tests, you can then provide a mock or stub implementation of the interface.

Here's an example of a function that's hard to test because it has a side effect:

```go
Copy
func SaveUser(user User) error {
db, err := sql.Open("mysql", "user:password@/database")
if err != nil {
return err
    }
defer db.Close()

_, err = db.Exec
("INSERT INTO users
(name, email) VALUES
(?, ?)", user.Name, user.Email)
    return err
}
```

This function saves a user to a database. However, it's hard to test because it opens a real database connection. In a test, we don't want to interact with a real database.

Here's how we could refactor this code to be more testable:

```go
type UserStore interface {
    Save(User) error
}

type MySQLUserStore struct {
    db *sql.DB
}

func (s *MySQLUserStore) Save(user User) error {
_, err := s.db.Exec("INSERT INTO users (name, email) VALUES (?, ?)", user.Name, user.Email)
    return err
}

func SaveUser(store UserStore, user User) error {
return store.Save(user)
}
```

Now, SaveUser takes a UserStore interface as a parameter. In production code, we can provide a MySQLUserStore that saves users to a real MySQL database. But in our tests, we can provide a mock UserStore that just records which users were saved:

```go
type MockUserStore struct {
users []User
}
```

```go
func (s *MockUserStore)
Save(user User) error {
s.users = append(s.users, user)
return nil
}

func TestSaveUser(t *testing.T) {
store := &MockUserStore{}
user := User{Name: "Alice", Email: "alice@example.com"}

err := SaveUser(store, user)
if err != nil {
t.Fatal(err)
    }

if len(store.users) != 1
  || store.users[0] != user {
t.Errorf("SaveUser didn't
 save the correct user")
    }
}
```

This test creates a MockUserStore and passes it to SaveUser. It then checks that the user was correctly recorded in the mock store.

By using an interface and providing a mock implementation in our tests, we've made SaveUser much easier to test.

Test Fixtures and Helper Functions

In many cases, you'll find yourself needing to set up some initial state for your tests, or performing the same operations in multiple tests. This is where test fixtures and helper functions come in.

A test fixture is a fixed state that exists at the start of a test. It's useful for setting up things like database connections, temporary directories, or mock objects.

In Go, you can define a test fixture by using a TestMain function:

```go
func TestMain(m *testing.M) {
// Set up test fixtures
    // ...

// Run tests
exitCode := m.Run()

// Clean up test fixtures
// ...

os.Exit(exitCode)
}
```

TestMain is called before any of the test functions are run. It's responsible for setting up any necessary state and cleaning it up after the tests are finished.

Helper functions are functions that perform common operations needed by multiple tests. They can help reduce duplication and make your tests more readable.

For example, let's say you have many tests that need to create a temporary file with some content:

```go
func TestSomething(t *testing.T) {
file, err := ioutil.TempFile("", "test")
if err != nil {
t.Fatal(err)
    }
defer os.Remove(file.Name())

_, err = file.Write([]byte("test content"))
if err != nil {
t.Fatal(err)
```

```go
    }
    // ...
}
```

You could move the temporary file creation into a helper function:

```go
Copy
func createTempFile
(t *testing.T, content string)
*os.File {
t.Helper()

file, err := ioutil.
TempFile("", "test")
if err != nil {
t.Fatal(err)
    }
t.Cleanup(func() {
os.Remove(file.Name())
    })

_, err = file.
Write([]byte(content))
if err != nil {
t.Fatal(err)
    }

    return file
}
```

Now your test can simply call createTempFile:

```go
Copy
func TestSomething
(t *testing.T) {
```

```
file := createTempFile
(t, "test content")
    // ...
}
```

This makes the test more readable and ensures that all temporary files are properly cleaned up.

Note the use of t.Helper() in the helper function. This tells the testing framework that this is a helper function, so if the test fails, the failure will be reported at the line where the helper was called, not inside the helper itself.

Also note the use of t.Cleanup. This registers a function to be called after the test is finished, whether it passes or fails. It's a convenient way to ensure that cleanup happens even if the test fails.

Benchmarking and Profiling

In addition to testing the correctness of your code, it's often important to ensure that it performs well. Go's testing package provides support for benchmarking and profiling your code.

Benchmarking

A benchmark is a test that measures the performance of a piece of code. In Go, you write a benchmark by creating a function with a name starting with Benchmark and taking a *testing.B parameter:

```go
Copy
func BenchmarkAdd(b *testing.B) {
for i := 0; i < b.N; i++ {
Add(2, 3)
    }
}
```

The benchmark function should run the code you want to measure in a loop b.N times. The testing framework will automatically adjust N until the benchmark runs for a stable duration.

To run benchmarks, use the go test -bench flag:

```
Copy
$ go test -bench .
goos: darwin
goarch: amd64
pkg: example/math
BenchmarkAdd-8
1000000000
0.279 ns/op
PASS
ok
example/math
0.330s
```

This output shows that BenchmarkAdd ran 1,000,000,000 times, and each operation took an average of 0.279 nanoseconds.

You can use benchmarks to compare the performance of different implementations or to track performance over time to catch regressions.

Profiling

Profiling is the process of analyzing your code to determine where it spends its time and memory. Go provides several profiling tools, including CPU profiling, memory profiling, and block profiling.

To enable profiling, you use flags with the go test command:

- -cpuprofile: Enables CPU profiling and writes the profile data to the specified file.
- -memprofile: Enables memory profiling and writes the profile data to the specified file.
- -blockprofile: Enables block profiling and writes the profile data to the

specified file.

For example, to perform CPU profiling on the BenchmarkAdd function:

```
Copy
$ go test -bench .
-cpuprofile cpu.prof
```

This runs the benchmarks and writes the CPU profile data to cpu.prof. To analyze the profile data, you can use the pprof tool:

```
Copy
$ go tool pprof cpu.prof
Type: cpu
Time: Jun 5, 2023 at
10:01am (EDT)
Duration: 2.17s,
Total samples =
1.92s (88.48%)
Entering interactive mode
(type "help" for commands,
"o" for options)
(pprof) top
Showing nodes accounting for
1.92s, 100% of 1.92s total
flat  flat%   sum%
 cum   cum%
1.92s  100%   100%
1.92s  100%   example/
math.BenchmarkAdd
0      0%     100%
1.92s  100%   example/math.
BenchmarkAdd.func1
0      0%     100%
1.92s  100%   testing.
(*B).launch
0      0%     100%
```

```
1.92s    100%
testing.(*B).runN
```

This output shows that 100% of the CPU time was spent in the BenchmarkAdd function.

You can use pprof interactively to explore the profile data in more detail, generate visualizations, and identify performance bottlenecks.

Profiling is a powerful tool for optimizing your code. By identifying the parts of your code that consume the most resources, you can focus your optimization efforts where they'll have the greatest impact.

Conclusion

Testing and benchmarking are essential practices for writing high-quality Go code. In this chapter, we've learned how to write tests using the testing package, how to structure our code to be more testable, how to use test fixtures and helper functions, and how to benchmark and profile our code.

Remember, tests are not a substitute for good design and thorough code reviews. But they are a valuable safety net that can catch bugs, prevent regressions, and give you the confidence to refactor and improve your code over time.

In the next chapter, we'll dive into another important topic for writing robust Go programs: debugging and error handling. We'll learn techniques for troubleshooting issues in our code, how to handle errors gracefully, and best practices for logging and monitoring in production environments. See you there!

Chapter 10: Debugging and Error Handling

Writing code is only half the battle. No matter how skilled you are, bugs and errors are inevitable. Being able to effectively debug and handle errors is just as important as writing the code in the first place.

In this chapter, we'll explore techniques and tools for debugging Go code, including the Delve debugger. We'll also dive into error handling in Go, covering the built-in error type, panic and recover, logging with the log package, and creating custom error types.

Debugging with Delve

Delve is a powerful open source debugger for Go. It allows you to pause the execution of your program, inspect variables, set breakpoints, and step through your code line by line.

To install Delve, use the go get command:

```
Copy
$ go get -u github.com/go-delve/delve/cmd/dlv
```

This will download and install the dlv command-line tool.

To start debugging a Go program with Delve, navigate to the directory containing your main package and run:

```
Copy
$ dlv debug
```

This will compile your program with debugging symbols and start the debugger.

Once in the debugger, you can use commands to control the execution of your program. Some common commands include:

- break or b: Set a breakpoint at a specific line or function.
- continue or c: Continue execution until the next breakpoint.
- next or n: Step over to the next line.
- step or s: Step into a function call.
- print or p: Print the value of a variable or expression.

For example, let's say we have a simple program:

```go
Copy
package main

func main() {
    x := 1
    y := 2
    z := x + y
    fmt.Println(z)
}
```

We can set a breakpoint on line 6 (z := x + y) by running:

CHAPTER 10: DEBUGGING AND ERROR HANDLING

```
Copy
(dlv) break 6
Breakpoint 1 set at 0x1087d9b
for main.main() ./main.go:6
```

Then we can run the program with continue:

```
Copy
(dlv) continue
> main.main() ./main.go:6
 (hits goroutine(1):1 total:1)
 (PC: 0x1087d9b)
     1: package main
     2:
3: func main() {
4:x := 1
5:y := 2
=>   6:z := x + y
7:fmt.Println(z)
8: }
```

The debugger pauses at line 6. We can inspect the values of x and y:

```
Copy
(dlv) print x
1
(dlv) print y
2
```

And we can step over to the next line with next:

```
Copy
(dlv) next
> main.main() ./main.go:7
(PC: 0x1087da6)
     2:
     3: func main() {
```

```
    4:     x := 1
    5:     y := 2
    6:     z := x + y
=>  7:     fmt.Println(z)
    8: }
```

Delve has many more features, including conditional breakpoints, attaching to running processes, and remote debugging. It's an essential tool for any Go developer's toolkit.

Handling Errors and Panics

In Go, errors are values. The built-in error type is an interface:

```go
Copy
type error interface {
    Error() string
}
```

Any type that has an Error method that returns a string implements the error interface and can be used as an error value.

By convention, functions in Go return an error value as their last return value. If the function succeeds, it returns nil for the error. If it fails, it returns a non-nil error.

Here's an example:

```go
Copy
func Divide(x, y int)
  (int, error) {
if y == 0 {
return 0, errors.
New("division by zero")
```

CHAPTER 10: DEBUGGING AND ERROR HANDLING

```
    }
    return x / y, nil
}
```

The caller of this function should always check the error before using the result:

```go
result, err := Divide(10, 2)
if err != nil {
    // handle the error
    return
}
// use the result
```

In addition to returning errors, Go also has a mechanism for handling unexpected or unrecoverable errors: panics. When a function panics, it immediately stops execution, unwinds the stack, and returns control to the first deferred function (if any).

You can cause a panic by calling the panic function with an error value:

```go
func foo() {
    panic("something went wrong")
}
```

You can handle a panic with the recover function. recover stops the unwinding process and returns the argument passed to panic. It's only useful inside deferred functions.

Here's an example:

```go
Copy
func foo() {
defer func() {
if r := recover(); r != nil {
fmt.Println
("Recovered from panic:", r)
        }
    }()

panic("something went wrong")
}

func main() {
foo()
fmt.Println
("Program continues normally")
}
```

In this example, foo panics, but the deferred anonymous function recovers from the panic. The program then continues normally.

It's important to note that you should only use panics for truly unexpected errors, like a bug in your code. For expected errors (like a file not existing), you should return an error value.

Logging with the log Package

When you're debugging or monitoring a program, it's often helpful to output logs - messages that record what the program is doing. Go's standard library includes the log package for simple logging.

Here's a basic example:

```go
Copy
package main
```

CHAPTER 10: DEBUGGING AND ERROR HANDLING

```
import "log"

func main() {
    log.Println("This is a log message")
}
```

This will output:

```
Copy
2023/06/05 11:22:33
This is a log message
```

The log package automatically prefixes each log message with a timestamp.

You can also use log.Printf to create formatted log messages, similar to fmt.Printf:

```go
Copy
log.Printf("The
  value of x is %d", x)
```

By default, the log package writes to standard error. You can change this by setting the output destination:

```go
Copy
log.SetOutput(os.Stdout)
```

You can also prefix each log message with additional information, like the file and line number where the log was written:

```go
Copy
```

```
log.SetFlags(log.Ldate
| log.Ltime | log.Lshortfile)
log.Println
("This is a log message")
```

This will output:

```
Copy
2023/06/05 11:25:01
 main.go:6:
This is a log message
```

The log package is simple but effective for basic logging needs. For more advanced logging, you might want to use a third-party package like logrus or zap.

Creating Custom Error Types

While you can create error values with errors.New, sometimes you want more structure to your errors. In these cases, you can define your own error types.

Here's an example:

```go
Copy
type DivisionError struct {
    IntA int
    IntB int
}

func (e *DivisionError)
 Error() string {
return fmt.Sprintf
("cannot divide %d by
 %d", e.IntA, e.IntB)
}
```

CHAPTER 10: DEBUGGING AND ERROR HANDLING

```go
func Divide(a, b int)
int, error) {
if b == 0 {
return 0, &DivisionError{a, b}
    }
return a / b, nil
}
```

In this example, we define a DivisionError struct that contains the integers that were being divided. We also implement the Error method on *Division-Error, which makes *DivisionError implement the error interface.

In the Divide function, instead of returning a plain error created with errors.New, we return a pointer to a DivisionError instance.

Now when we call Divide, we can check for the specific DivisionError:

```go
Copy
result, err := Divide(10, 0)
if err != nil {
if de, ok := err.
(*DivisionError); ok {
fmt.Printf
("Tried to divide %d by %d\n",
 de.IntA, de.IntB)
    } else {
// handle other errors
    }
    return
}
```

We use a type assertion to check if the error is a *DivisionError. If it is, we can access the IntA and IntB fields.

Creating custom error types allows you to add more context and meaning to your errors. It can make your error handling more precise and informative.

Conclusion

Debugging and error handling are critical skills for any Go developer. In this chapter, we've learned how to use the Delve debugger to inspect and control the execution of our programs. We've also explored Go's built-in error handling mechanisms, including the error interface, returning errors from functions, panics and recover, logging with the log package, and creating custom error types.

Remember, the goal of debugging and error handling is not just to fix bugs, but to understand why they occurred and to prevent them from happening again. By using tools like Delve and techniques like structured error handling, you can gain deeper insight into your code and write more robust, reliable programs.

In the next chapter, we'll dive into some of Go's more advanced language features, including generics, reflection, unsafe code, and calling C libraries with cgo. These features can be powerful tools in certain situations, but they also come with their own challenges and gotchas. We'll learn when and how to use them effectively. See you there!

Chapter 11: Advanced Language Features

In the previous chapters, we've covered the fundamental features of Go that you'll use in most of your programs. However, Go also has some more advanced features that can be very powerful in certain situations. In this chapter, we'll explore four of these advanced features: generics, reflection, unsafe code, and calling C libraries with cgo. These features can help you write more flexible, dynamic, and performant code, but they also come with their own challenges and best practices. We'll learn when and how to use them effectively.

Generics

Go 1.18 introduced support for generics, also known as parametric polymorphism. Generics allow you to write code that is abstract over types, enabling you to create functions and data structures that work with different types without duplication.

Before generics, if you wanted to write a function that could operate on slices of different types, you'd have to write separate functions for each type:

```go
Copy
func SumInts(nums []int) int {
```

```go
    var sum int
    for _, num := range nums {
        sum += num
    }
    return sum
}

func SumFloats(nums []float64) float64 {
    var sum float64
    for _, num := range nums {
        sum += num
    }
    return sum
}
```

With generics, you can write a single function that works with any slice type:

```go
Copy
func SumIntsOrFloats[T int | float64](nums []T) T {
    var sum T
    for _, num := range nums {
        sum += num
    }
    return sum
}
```

The T in square brackets is a type parameter. It represents a placeholder for a concrete type that will be provided when the function is called. The int | float64 after the type parameter is a type constraint, which specifies what types can be used in place of T. Here, T can be either int or float64.

You can call this function with a slice of int or float64:

```go
Copy
```

CHAPTER 11: ADVANCED LANGUAGE FEATURES

```
ints := []int{1, 2, 3}
floats := []float64
{1.0, 2.0, 3.0}

fmt.Println
(SumIntsOrFloats(ints))
 // Output: 6
fmt.Println(SumIntsOrFloats
(floats)) // Output: 6.0
```

Generics can also be used with structs and interfaces. Here's an example of a generic struct:

```go
Copy
type Stack[T any] struct {
    items []T
}

func (s *Stack[T])
 Push(item T) {
s.items = append
(s.items, item)
}

func (s *Stack[T])
Pop() (T, bool) {
if len(s.items) == 0 {
var zero T
return zero, false
    }
item := s.items[len(s.items)-1]
s.items = s.items
[:len(s.items)-1]
return item, true
}
```

This Stack struct can hold elements of any type T. The any keyword is a predeclared identifier that is an alias for the empty interface type interface{}, meaning it can represent any type.

You can create instances of Stack with different element types:

```go
Copy
intStack := &Stack[int]{}
intStack.Push(1)
intStack.Push(2)
fmt.Println(intStack.Pop()) // Output: 2 true

stringStack := &Stack[string]{}
stringStack.Push("hello")
stringStack.Push("world")
fmt.Println(stringStack.Pop()) // Output: world true
```

Generics are a powerful feature that can help you write more reusable and expressive code. However, they can also make your code more complex and harder to understand. Use them judiciously, and always consider whether a simpler, non-generic solution would suffice.

Reflection

Reflection in Go is the ability of a program to examine its own structure and behavior at runtime. It's provided by the reflect package.

With reflection, you can inspect the type and value of a variable, modify values dynamically, call functions and methods by name, and more. This can be very useful for creating flexible and dynamic systems, such as serialization frameworks, dependency injection containers, and plugin systems.

Here's a simple example that demonstrates inspecting a value with reflection:

```go
Copy
```

CHAPTER 11: ADVANCED LANGUAGE FEATURES

```go
func Inspect(x interface{}) {
v := reflect.ValueOf(x)
t := v.Type()

fmt.Printf("Type: %v\n", t)
fmt.Printf
("Kind: %v\n", v.Kind())
fmt.Printf
("Value: %v\n",
 v.Interface())
}

func main() {
    x := 42
    Inspect(x)
}
```

Output:

```
Copy
Type: int
Kind: int
Value: 42
```

The Inspect function takes an interface{} value, which can hold a value of any type. It then uses reflect.ValueOf to get a reflect.Value representing the value, and reflect.TypeOf (or the Type method of reflect.Value) to get a reflect.Type representing its type.

The Kind method of reflect.Value returns a reflect.Kind, which is a constant representing the specific kind of value (e.g., int, float64, string, slice, map, struct).

The Interface method of reflect.Value returns an interface{} value holding the actual value.

Reflection can also be used to modify values:

```go
func DoubleAt
(x interface{}, i int) {
v := reflect.ValueOf(x)
if v.Kind() != reflect.
Ptr || v.Elem().
Kind() != reflect.Slice {
panic("DoubleAt
called with non-
pointer-to-slice")
    }

slice := v.Elem()
if i < 0 || i >=
slice.Len() {
panic("DoubleAt
called with out-of-bounds index")
    }

elem := slice.Index(i)
if elem.Kind() != reflect.Int {
panic("DoubleAt
called with non-int
slice element")
    }

elem.SetInt(elem.Int() * 2)
}

func main() {
xs := []int{1, 2, 3}
DoubleAt(&xs, 1)
fmt.Println(xs)
// Output: [1 4 3]
}
```

The DoubleAt function expects a pointer to a slice of int. It checks this using the Kind method. It then gets the underlying slice value with Elem, checks the index bounds, gets the element at the given index with Index, and doubles

CHAPTER 11: ADVANCED LANGUAGE FEATURES

its value with SetInt.

Note that to modify a value with reflection, you need to have a reflect.Value that is addressable (i.e., it represents a variable or a pointer to a variable, not a literal or computed value). That's why DoubleAt takes a pointer.

Reflection is a complex and powerful feature, and there's much more to it than we can cover here. However, it's important to note that reflection should be used sparingly, as it can make your code harder to understand and maintain, and it can circumvent the type safety and performance optimizations of the Go compiler. Always consider whether there's a simpler, non-reflective way to achieve your goal.

Unsafe Code

Go is a type-safe language, which means that the compiler enforces strict rules about how values of different types can interact. However, sometimes you need to bypass these rules and interact with memory directly. That's where the unsafe package comes in.

The unsafe package provides operations that step around the type safety of Go programs. These include:

- unsafe.Pointer: a pointer type that can hold the address of any variable
- unsafe.Sizeof: a function that returns the size in bytes of a value
- unsafe.Alignof: a function that returns the alignment of a value
- unsafe.Offsetof: a function that returns the offset of a field within a struct

Here's an example that uses unsafe.Pointer to interpret the bytes of a string as a []byte:

```go
Copy
func StringToBytes(s string) []byte {
var b []byte
hdr := (*reflect.
```

```go
SliceHeader)(unsafe.Pointer(&b))
hdr.Data = (*reflect.StringHeader)(unsafe.Pointer(&s)).Data
hdr.Len = len(s)
hdr.Cap = len(s)
    return b
}

func main() {
s := "hello"
b := StringToBytes(s)
fmt.Println(b) //
 Output: [104 101 108 108 111]
}
```

In this example, we create a []byte variable b, and then use unsafe.Pointer to get a pointer to its underlying reflect.SliceHeader. We then set the Data field of this header to the Data field of the reflect.StringHeader of the string s, effectively making b point to the same underlying bytes as s. Finally, we set the Len and Cap fields to the length of s.

This conversion works because the in-memory representation of a string is a pointer to a byte array and a length, which is exactly the same as the representation of a []byte. However, it's important to note that modifying the bytes of a string in this way is undefined behavior, as strings are supposed to be immutable in Go.

Unsafe code should be used with extreme caution, as it can easily introduce hard-to-find bugs, portability issues, and security vulnerabilities. It should only be used when absolutely necessary, such as when interacting with C libraries or implementing low-level data structures.

Cgo and Calling C Libraries

Go provides excellent support for calling C code and linking against C libraries through a feature called cgo. Cgo allows you to include C code directly in your Go source files, and to call C functions and use C types from your Go code.

CHAPTER 11: ADVANCED LANGUAGE FEATURES

Here's a simple example of calling a C function from Go:

```go
package main

/*
#include <stdio.h>

void hello() {
    printf("Hello, World!\n");
}
*/
import "C"

func main() {
    C.hello()
}
```

In this example, the C code is included directly in the Go source file, surrounded by /* and */ comment delimiters. The import "C" statement is a special import that makes the C code available to the Go code.

The main function simply calls the C hello function, which prints "Hello, World!" to the console.

Cgo also allows you to define Go functions that can be called from C code, and to use C types in your Go code. For example:

```go
package main

/*
#include <stdio.h>

extern void goPrint(char*);

void cPrint(char* s) {
```

```
printf("%s\n", s);
goPrint("Hello from C!");
}
*/
import "C"

import "fmt"

//export goPrint
func goPrint(s *C.char) {
fmt.Println(C.GoString(s))
}

func main() {
C.cPrint(C.CString
("Hello from Go!"))
}
```

In this example, the C code defines a cPrint function that takes a char* (a C string). It prints this string, and then calls a goPrint function, which is expected to be defined in the Go code.

The Go code defines the goPrint function, which takes a *C.char (a pointer to a C string). The //export comment makes this function available to C code. The function uses C.GoString to convert the C string to a Go string, and then prints it.

The main function calls the C cPrint function, passing it a C string created with C.CString.

Cgo is a powerful feature that allows you to leverage existing C libraries and to write performance-critical code in C while still enjoying the benefits of Go's memory safety and concurrency features. However, it also introduces complexity and can make your code harder to port and maintain. Use it judiciously, and always consider whether a pure-Go solution would suffice.

Conclusion

In this chapter, we've explored some of Go's more advanced language features: generics, reflection, unsafe code, and cgo. These features can be very powerful in certain situations, but they also come with their own challenges and best practices.

Generics allow you to write code that is abstract over types, enabling more code reuse and expressiveness. Reflection allows you to inspect and manipulate the structure and behavior of your program at runtime, enabling more dynamic and flexible systems. Unsafe code allows you to bypass Go's type safety and interact with memory directly, enabling performance optimizations and interoperability with C. Cgo allows you to call C code and link against C libraries from your Go code, enabling leverage of existing C ecosystems.

However, each of these features also introduces complexity and potential pitfalls. Generics can make your code harder to understand and debug. Reflection can circumvent the type safety and performance optimizations of the compiler. Unsafe code can introduce subtle bugs and security vulnerabilities. Cgo can make your code harder to port and maintain.

As with any advanced feature, the key is to use them judiciously and appropriately. Always consider whether a simpler, more idiomatic solution would suffice. When you do use these features, do so with care and with a clear understanding of the trade-offs involved.

And with that, we come to the end of our journey through the Go programming language. We've covered a lot of ground, from the basics of the language to advanced topics like concurrency, testing, and unsafe code. I hope this book has given you a solid foundation in Go and the confidence to tackle real-world problems with it.

Remember, learning a programming language is just the beginning. The real journey is in applying that knowledge to build useful, reliable, and efficient software. Go forth and build amazing things!

Chapter 12: Deploying Go Applications

In the previous chapters, we've focused on writing Go code and building applications. But once you've built your application, how do you get it into the hands of your users?

In this final chapter, we'll explore the process of deploying Go applications. We'll cover compiling your code for different platforms, containerizing your application with Docker, deploying to various cloud platforms, and automating your deployment process with continuous integration and delivery.

Compiling for Different Platforms

One of the great advantages of Go is that it supports cross-compilation. This means you can compile your Go code on one platform (say, your development machine running macOS) and produce a binary that can run on another platform (say, a Linux server).

To cross-compile, you set the GOOS and GOARCH environment variables before running go build. GOOS specifies the target operating system (e.g., linux, windows, darwin), and GOARCH specifies the target architecture (e.g., amd64, arm64).

For example, to compile a binary for 64-bit Linux:

CHAPTER 12: DEPLOYING GO APPLICATIONS

```bash
Copy
GOOS=linux GOARCH=amd64 go build
```

This will produce a binary that can run on a 64-bit Linux system, regardless of the system you compiled it on.

You can also set these variables for an individual command using the -o flag:

```bash
Copy
go build -o myapp-linux-amd64
```

This will output the binary with a name that includes the target OS and architecture.

Go supports a wide variety of target OS/architecture combinations, including:

- linux/386
- linux/amd64
- linux/arm
- linux/arm64
- windows/386
- windows/amd64
- darwin/amd64
- darwin/arm64

and many more. See the documentation for the full list.

When deploying to a server or a cloud platform, you'll typically want to compile your binary for the target system's OS and architecture. Many CI/CD systems (which we'll discuss later) can automate this process for you.

Containerizing with Docker

In modern application deployment, it's common to package your application and its dependencies into a container. Containers provide a lightweight, portable, and reproducible way to distribute and run your application.

Docker is the most popular container platform. It allows you to define your application and its environment in a Dockerfile, which you can then use to build a container image.

Here's an example Dockerfile for a Go application:

```dockerfile
Copy
# Start from the official
 Golang base image
FROM golang:1.20 as builder

# Set the working directory
WORKDIR /app

# Copy go.mod and go.sum
files to the workspace
COPY go.mod go.sum ./

# Download dependencies
RUN go mod download

# Copy the rest of the source code
COPY . .

# Build the application
RUN CGO_ENABLED=0 GOOS=
linux go build -o main .

# Start a new stage from scratch
FROM alpine:latest
RUN apk --no-cache
add ca-certificates
```

CHAPTER 12: DEPLOYING GO APPLICATIONS

```
WORKDIR /root/

# Copy the binary from the builder stage
COPY --from=builder /app/main .

# Expose the application's
port (adjust if necessary)
EXPOSE 8080

# Run the binary
CMD ["./main"]
```

This Dockerfile does the following:

1. It starts from the official Go base image.
2. It sets the working directory to /app.
3. It copies go.mod and go.sum and downloads the dependencies. This is done as a separate step to take advantage of Docker's layer caching - if your dependencies don't change, Docker can reuse this layer from a previous build.
4. It copies the rest of the source code.
5. It builds the application, setting CGO_ENABLED=0 (to produce a statically linked binary) and GOOS=linux (to produce a Linux binary regardless of the host system).
6. It starts a new stage from the alpine base image (a minimal Linux distribution).
7. It copies the binary from the previous stage.
8. It exposes the application's port.
9. It specifies the command to run when the container starts.

You can build a Docker image from this Dockerfile with:

bash
Copy

```
docker build -t myapp .
```

And then run a container from this image with:

```bash
Copy
docker run -p 8080:8080 myapp
```

This will start your application in a container, mapping the container's port 8080 to the host's port 8080.

Containerizing your application has many benefits:

- It ensures that your application runs in the same environment everywhere, eliminating "works on my machine" problems.
- It makes your application portable - you can run it anywhere that Docker is installed, whether that's your local machine, a server, or a cloud platform.
- It simplifies your deployment process - you just need to build the container image and then run it.

Many cloud platforms and orchestration systems (like Kubernetes) are designed around containers, so containerizing your application is often a necessary step for deploying to these platforms.

Deploying to Cloud Platforms

Cloud platforms like Amazon Web Services (AWS), Google Cloud Platform (GCP), and Microsoft Azure offer a wide variety of services for deploying and running applications. Go is well-supported on all major cloud platforms.

The exact process for deploying a Go application will depend on the specific platform and service you're using, but the general steps are:

1. Compile your application for the target platform.

2. Package your application (e.g., in a container or a zip file).
3. Upload your application to the cloud platform.
4. Configure the service to run your application.

For example, to deploy a Go application to AWS Elastic Beanstalk (a service for running web applications):

1. Compile your application for linux/amd64.
2. Create a Dockerfile for your application (as shown in the previous section).
3. Create a .elasticbeanstalk directory in your project and add a config.yml file that specifies the Docker platform:

```yaml
Copy
deploy:
  artifact: Dockerrun.aws.json
```

1. Create a Dockerrun.aws.json file in your project that specifies your Docker image:

```json
Copy
{
  "AWSEBDockerrunVersion": "1",
  "Image": {
    "Name": "myapp",
    "Update": "true"
  },
  "Ports": [
    {
      "ContainerPort": "8080"
```

```
    }
  ]
}
```

1. Use the AWS CLI to create a new Elastic Beanstalk application and environment:

```bash
Copy
eb init -p docker myapp
eb create myapp-env
```

1. Use the AWS CLI to deploy your application:

```bash
Copy
eb deploy
```

This will build your Docker image, upload it to AWS, and start running your application in Elastic Beanstalk.

Other cloud platforms have similar services and workflows. For example, Google Cloud Run allows you to run stateless containers, and Azure App Service supports deploying Docker containers.

In addition to these platform-specific services, you can also use container orchestration systems like Kubernetes to deploy and manage your applications on any cloud platform (or even on your own infrastructure). Kubernetes provides a uniform way to deploy, scale, and manage containerized applications.

Deploying to a cloud platform offers many benefits, such as scalability, reliability, and reduced operational overhead. However, it also introduces new complexities, such as choosing the right services, configuring them correctly, and managing costs. It's important to familiarize yourself with your chosen platform's best practices and to start with a simple deployment before gradually adding more components and services.

Continuous Integration and Delivery

Continuous Integration (CI) and Continuous Delivery (CD) are practices that automate the building, testing, and deployment of applications.

In a typical CI/CD workflow, whenever a developer pushes code to the repository, the CI system automatically builds the code and runs the tests. If the build and tests pass, the CD system then deploys the application to a staging or production environment.

There are many CI/CD systems available, both as hosted services and as self-hosted software. Some popular options include:

- Jenkins
- Travis CI
- CircleCI
- GitHub Actions
- GitLab CI/CD
- AWS CodePipeline
- Google Cloud Build

Setting up a CI/CD system typically involves:

1. Configuring your repository to trigger the CI/CD system when code is pushed.
2. Writing a configuration file that tells the CI/CD system how to build, test, and deploy your application.
3. Configuring the target environment where your application will be deployed.

For example, here's a simple GitHub Actions workflow that builds and tests a Go application:

```yaml
Copy
name: CI

on:
  push:
branches: [ main ]
pull_request:
branches: [ main ]

jobs:

  build:
runs-on: ubuntu-latest

    steps:
- uses: actions/checkout@v3

- name: Set up Go
uses: actions/setup-go@v3
with:
go-version: 1.20

- name: Build
run: go build -v ./...

- name: Test
run: go test -v ./...
```

This workflow does the following:

1. It triggers on pushes and pull requests to the main branch.
2. It checks out the code.
3. It sets up Go.
4. It builds the application.
5. It runs the tests.

You could extend this workflow to also deploy the application if the build and tests pass:

```yaml
Copy
    - name: Deploy
if: success() && github.ref
  == 'refs/heads/main'
run: |
# Your deployment steps here
# For example, you might
build a Docker
image and push it to a registry
```

Using a CI/CD system has many benefits:

- It automates repetitive tasks, reducing the chance of human error.
- It ensures that tests are run on every change, catching bugs early.
- It enables frequent, small deployments, which are less risky than large, infrequent ones.
- It provides a consistent and reproducible deployment process.

Implementing CI/CD can be challenging, especially for complex applications with many dependencies and environments. It requires a significant upfront investment in automation and configuration. However, the long-term benefits in terms of reliability, agility, and developer productivity are substantial.

Conclusion

Deploying applications is a complex and multifaceted topic, but it's a critical part of the software development lifecycle. In this chapter, we've covered some of the key aspects of deploying Go applications:

- Cross-compiling for different platforms

- Containerizing applications with Docker
- Deploying to cloud platforms
- Automating the deployment process with CI/CD

Each of these topics could fill a book on its own, but this chapter should give you a starting point and an overview of the landscape.

Remember, there's no one "right" way to deploy an application. The best approach will depend on your specific application, your team, your infrastructure, and your business requirements. It's important to start simple, iterate, and continuously improve your deployment process.

With the knowledge you've gained from this book, you're well-equipped to build, test, and deploy robust and efficient Go applications. Go's simplicity, performance, and strong ecosystem make it an excellent choice for a wide variety of applications and environments.

As you continue your Go journey, keep learning, keep experimenting, and keep sharing your knowledge with others. The Go community is known for its inclusivity, pragmatism, and helpfulness - don't hesitate to reach out for help or to contribute back to the ecosystem.

Thank you for reading this book. I hope it has been helpful and that it has inspired you to build great things with Go. Happy coding!

Section IV: Go in the Real World Chapter 13: Interviews with Go Experts

In this final section of the book, we'll explore how Go is being used in the real world. We'll hear from experts who are using Go to build innovative applications and solve complex problems. We'll also take a look at the broader Go ecosystem, including the tools, libraries, and community resources that are available to Go developers.

Chapter 13: Interviews with Go Experts

One of the best ways to understand how Go is being used in practice is to hear directly from the people who are using it. In this chapter, we've interviewed two Go experts who are using the language in different ways and in different domains.

Expert 1: Jane Smith, Senior Software Engineer at Acme Inc.

<img src="/api/placeholder/200/200" alt="placeholder" />

Jane Smith is a senior software engineer at Acme Inc., where she leads the development of a large-scale distributed system that processes millions of transactions per day. She has been working with Go for over five years and has become a vocal advocate for the language.

Q: What led you to start using Go?

A: I was working on a project that required high concurrency and low latency, and we were struggling to achieve the performance we needed with our existing stack. We evaluated several languages and frameworks, and Go stood out for its simplicity, performance, and built-in concurrency primitives. We decided to give it a try, and we were immediately impressed by how easy it was to write efficient, concurrent code in Go.

Q: What do you think are the strongest features of Go?

A: For me, the strongest features of Go are its simplicity and its performance. The language is very minimal and easy to learn, but it still provides all the features you need to write robust, efficient code. The performance is also excellent - we've been able to achieve very low latency and high throughput with Go, even under heavy load.

I also really appreciate the standard library and the tooling around Go. The standard library provides a lot of functionality out of the box, and the tools like go fmt, go test, and go build make it easy to maintain a consistent, high-quality codebase.

Q: How does Go compare to other languages you've used?

A: I've used a lot of different languages over the years, including C++, Java, Python, and Ruby. Compared to these languages, I find Go to be much simpler and more focused. It doesn't have a lot of the bells and whistles that some other languages have, but that's actually a good thing - it means there's less to learn and less to go wrong.

At the same time, Go is still a very powerful language. It has excellent support for concurrency, a robust type system, and a lot of other features that make it suitable for a wide range of applications. It's not the right choice for every project, but for the kind of systems programming and network services that we build at Acme, it's a great fit.

Q: What advice would you give to someone who is just starting to learn Go?

A: My advice would be to focus on the fundamentals. Go is a simple language, but it still has a lot of depth. Take the time to really understand the core concepts like goroutines, channels, and interfaces. Write a lot of small programs to practice using these features.

I would also encourage new Go developers to get involved in the community. The Go community is very welcoming and supportive, and there are a lot of great resources available, like the Go forum, the Gopher Slack, and the many Go conferences and meetups around the world.

Finally, don't be afraid to ask for help when you need it. Go has a strong culture of mentorship and collaboration, and there are always people who are willing to lend a hand or answer a question.

Expert 2: John Doe, CTO at Beta LLC

John Doe is the CTO at Beta LLC, a startup that is building a next-generation machine learning platform. He has been using Go since the early days of the language and has built several successful products and libraries with it.

Q: What kind of applications are you building with Go at Beta?

A: At Beta, we're using Go to build the backend services for our machine learning platform. This includes things like data ingestion pipelines, feature engineering workflows, model training and serving infrastructure, and more.

We chose Go for these components because of its performance and its suitability for building large-scale distributed systems. We need to be able to process a lot of data very quickly, and Go's concurrency features and efficient memory model make it a great fit for this kind of workload.

Q: What libraries or tools do you use with Go?

A: We use a lot of the standard Go libraries, especially things like net/http for building web services, encoding/json for working with JSON data, and database/sql for interacting with databases.

We also use a number of third-party libraries. Some of our favorites include:

- gorm for database ORM
- gin for building REST APIs
- cobra for building CLI tools

- testify for writing unit tests
- prometheus for monitoring and metrics

In terms of tools, we rely heavily on the standard Go toolchain, including go build, go test, and go fmt. We also use golangci-lint for static code analysis and gocover for measuring test coverage.

Q: How do you handle dependencies in your Go projects?

A: We use Go modules for dependency management. We find modules to be a significant improvement over the older GOPATH-based approach. Modules make it easy to specify and version the dependencies for each project, and they ensure that everyone on the team is using the same versions of each library.

We also make heavy use of semantic versioning for our own libraries and applications. We follow the standard practices of using Git tags to mark releases and incrementing the major, minor, or patch version numbers as appropriate.

Q: What challenges have you encountered while using Go?

A: One of the biggest challenges we've encountered is managing the complexity of our distributed systems. Even with Go's concurrency features, it can be difficult to reason about the behavior of a complex system with many moving parts.

To address this, we've invested heavily in observability and monitoring. We use tools like Prometheus and Grafana to collect metrics and visualize the behavior of our systems. We also make extensive use of logging and tracing to help us debug issues when they arise.

Another challenge we've faced is the lack of generics in Go. While Go's type system is very powerful, there are some cases where generics would allow us to write more reusable and maintainable code. However, with the introduction of generics in Go 1.18, this is becoming less of an issue.

Q: What's your favorite thing about working with Go?

A: My favorite thing about Go is its simplicity and readability. Go code is very easy to understand, even if you're not the original author. This makes it much easier to collaborate with other developers and to maintain a codebase over time.

I also appreciate Go's emphasis on pragmatism and simplicity. The language designers have made a conscious choice to keep the language small and focused, and to prioritize practical concerns like performance, reliability, and maintainability over more academic or esoteric features.

Finally, I really enjoy being part of the Go community. The community is very friendly and inclusive, and there's a strong emphasis on collaboration and knowledge sharing. Whether you're a seasoned Go developer or just getting started, there's always someone who's willing to help out or share their experience.

Conclusion

These interviews provide a glimpse into how Go is being used in the real world to build complex, high-performance systems. While the specific use cases and challenges may vary, there are some common themes that emerge.

Go's simplicity, performance, and built-in concurrency features make it a great fit for building large-scale distributed systems and network services. The language's readability and maintainability also make it well-suited for collaborative development and long-term maintenance.

At the same time, Go's simplicity and focus on pragmatism mean that it may not be the best choice for every project. As with any technology choice, it's important to carefully consider the specific needs and constraints of your project before deciding to use Go.

Regardless of whether you choose to use Go for your next project, the insights and experiences shared by these experts provide valuable lessons and best practices that can be applied to any development effort. By focusing on simplicity, collaborating with others, and continuously learning and improving, we can all build better software and contribute to the wider community of developers.

Chapter 14: Go Best Practices and Idioms

In the previous chapter, we heard from Go experts about their experiences using the language in real-world applications. In this chapter, we'll dive into some of the best practices and idioms that have emerged in the Go community over the years.

These practices and idioms are not hard and fast rules, but rather guidelines and recommendations based on the collective experience of the Go community. By following these practices, you can write Go code that is more readable, maintainable, and idiomatic.

Naming Conventions

One of the first things you'll notice when reading Go code is that it has a distinctive style and set of conventions for naming. These conventions are not just a matter of personal preference, but are actually enforced by the Go compiler and tools.

Capitalization

In Go, the capitalization of a name determines its visibility outside the package. Names that start with a capital letter are exported, which means they can be used by other packages. Names that start with a lowercase letter are unexported, which means they are only visible within the same package.

For example:

```go
// exported
type User struct { ... }
func NewUser(name string) *User { ... }

// unexported
type config struct { ... }
func loadConfig() { ... }
```

This convention applies to all named entities in Go, including variables, functions, types, and constants.

Acronyms

Go conventions for acronyms are a bit different from some other languages. In Go, acronyms are usually written in all caps, regardless of their position in a name.

For example:

```go
type HTTPClient struct { ... }
func (c *HTTPClient) DoRequest
(url string) { ... }

type JSONEncoder struct { ... }
func (e *JSONEncoder)
Encode(v interface{})
  error { ... }
```

This convention can take some getting used to, especially if you're accustomed to camelCase or PascalCase naming styles. But it's an important part of writing idiomatic Go code.

Method Names

In Go, methods are functions that are associated with a particular type. When naming methods, the convention is to use a verb or verb phrase that describes the action of the method.

For example:

```go
Copy
type User struct { ... }

func (u *User) Save() error { ... }
func (u *User) Delete() error { ... }
func (u *User) SendEmail(subject, body string) error { ... }
```

This convention makes it clear what the method does and helps to keep method names concise and action-oriented.

Package Names

Package names in Go should be short, concise, and lowercase. They should also be singular, not plural.

For example:

```go
Copy
package user
package httputil
package json
```

Avoid package names that are too generic or too specific. The name should describe the purpose of the package without being overly broad or narrow.

Code Organization and Project Structure

Go has a unique approach to code organization and project structure. Unlike some languages that use a hierarchical directory structure based on namespaces or modules, Go uses a flat directory structure based on packages.

Package Organization

In Go, each directory corresponds to a package. The name of the directory is usually the same as the name of the package, although this is not required.

A typical Go project might have a structure like this:

```
Copy
myproject/
    main.go
    config/
        config.go
    handlers/
        handlers.go
    models/
        user.go
        post.go
    utils/
        utils.go
```

In this structure, each directory (config, handlers, models, utils) corresponds to a package. The main.go file in the root directory is the entry point for the application.

It's common to have a cmd directory for command-line tools and a pkg directory for shared packages that are used by multiple parts of the application.

Internal Packages

Go has a special convention for packages that are intended to be used only within a specific project or module. These are called "internal" packages.

An internal package is placed in a directory named internal or in a subdirectory of a directory named internal. This signals to the Go compiler and tools that the package should not be imported by code outside the parent directory of internal.

For example:

```
Copy
myproject/
    internal/
        config/
            config.go
    handlers/
        handlers.go
```

In this structure, the config package is an internal package that can only be imported by code in the myproject directory or its subdirectories. This is a useful way to encapsulate implementation details and prevent other parts of the application from depending on them directly.

Organizing Tests

Go has a built-in testing framework and a convention for organizing test files. Test files are placed in the same directory as the code they are testing and have a name ending in _test.go.

For example:

```
Copy
myproject/
    handlers/
        handlers.go
```

```
handlers_test.go
```

In this structure, the handlers_test.go file contains tests for the code in handlers.go.

It's also common to have a separate tests directory for integration tests or end-to-end tests that exercise multiple packages together.

Error Handling Best Practices

Error handling is an important part of writing robust and maintainable Go code. Go has a unique approach to error handling that emphasizes explicit error checking and propagation.

Returning Errors

In Go, it's conventional for functions to return an error as their last return value. If the function succeeds, it returns nil for the error. If it fails, it returns a non-nil error value.

For example:

```go
Copy
func DoSomething() error {
    err := doStep1()
    if err != nil {
        return err
    }

    err = doStep2()
    if err != nil {
        return err
    }

    return nil
}
```

This pattern allows the caller of the function to explicitly check for errors and handle them appropriately.

Error Types

Go's standard library defines an error interface that is used for representing errors:

```go
Copy
type error interface {
    Error() string
}
```

Any type that has an Error() string method satisfies this interface and can be used as an error value.

It's common to define custom error types for specific kinds of errors. These types often include additional information about the error, such as a code or a message.

For example:

```go
Copy
type NotFoundError struct {
    Name string
}

func (e *NotFoundError) Error() string {
    return fmt.Sprintf("%s not found", e.Name)
}
```

Custom error types make it possible to handle different kinds of errors in different ways and to convey more information about what went wrong.

Error Wrapping

When an error is passed up the call stack, it's often useful to add additional context to the error. This is called "error wrapping".

Go's standard library includes an errors package that provides functions for creating and wrapping errors. The fmt.Errorf function is also commonly used for this purpose.

For example:

```go
func DoSomething() error {
    err := doStep1()
    if err != nil {
        return fmt.Errorf
        ("failed to do step 1:
         %v", err)
    }

    err = doStep2()
    if err != nil {
        return fmt.Errorf
        ("failed to do step 2:
         %v", err)
    }

    return nil
}
```

This pattern allows errors to be propagated up the call stack with additional context at each level, making it easier to understand and debug errors.

Handling Errors

When an error is returned by a function, it's important to handle it appropriately. This might mean logging the error, returning it to the caller, or taking some corrective action.

One common pattern is to use a switch statement to handle different types of errors differently:

```go
Copy
err := DoSomething()
switch err := err.(type) {
case nil:
// success, no error
case *NotFoundError:
// handle not found error
case *PermissionError:
// handle permission error
default:
// handle unknown error
}
```

This pattern allows different types of errors to be handled in different ways, based on their type.

It's also important to consider when to handle errors and when to propagate them. As a general rule, errors should be handled at the level where there's enough context to make a decision about what to do. Lower-level functions should usually propagate errors up to higher-level functions that have more context.

Performance Tips and Tricks

Go is designed to be a fast and efficient language, with a focus on simplicity and performance. However, there are still ways to write Go code that is more performant and efficient.

Allocation

One of the most important factors in Go performance is allocation. Every time you create a new object, whether it's a struct, a slice, or a map, it requires an allocation. Allocations are relatively expensive, so it's important to minimize them where possible.

One way to reduce allocations is to reuse objects instead of creating new ones. For example, instead of creating a new slice every time you need one, you can reuse an existing slice by clearing it or resizing it.

```go
Copy
var buf []byte
for {
buf = buf[:0] // reuse
the slice by clearing it
n, err := r.Read(buf)
    // ...
}
```

Another way to reduce allocations is to use value types instead of pointer types where possible. Passing a value type (such as a struct or an array) as an argument to a function is more efficient than passing a pointer, because it doesn't require an allocation.

Concurrency

Go's concurrency primitives, goroutines and channels, are designed to be lightweight and efficient. However, there are still some best practices to follow to ensure that your concurrent code is performant.

One common mistake is to create too many goroutines. While goroutines are cheap compared to threads in other languages, they still have some overhead. Creating too many goroutines can lead to excessive context switching and can actually slow down your program.

As a general rule, you should only create as many goroutines as you need to keep all of your CPUs busy. The GOMAXPROCS environment variable or the runtime.GOMAXPROCS function can be used to control the number of operating system threads that can execute Go code simultaneously.

Another best practice is to use channels for communication between goroutines, rather than sharing memory. Channels provide a safe and efficient way to pass data between goroutines without the need for explicit locking.

However, it's important to be careful with buffered channels. A buffered channel can hold a certain number of values before the sender blocks. If the buffer is full, the sender will block until a value is removed from the buffer by the receiver. This can lead to unexpected behavior and can be a source of bugs.

Profiling and Benchmarking

To optimize the performance of your Go code, it's important to profile and benchmark it. Go provides built-in tools for profiling and benchmarking, including the pprof package and the testing package.

The pprof package allows you to profile the CPU usage, memory usage, and blocking behavior of your Go code. You can use it to identify performance bottlenecks and to understand how your code is using resources.

The testing package provides support for writing unit tests and benchmarks. Benchmarks are functions that measure the performance of a piece of code. You can use benchmarks to compare the performance of different implementations or to track performance over time.

For example:

```go
Copy
func BenchmarkFoo(b *testing.B) {
for i := 0; i < b.N; i++ {
Foo()
    }
}
```

This benchmark function measures the performance of the Foo function by calling it b.N times. The testing package automatically adjusts b.N until the benchmark runs for a stable duration.

By using profiling and benchmarking regularly, you can ensure that your Go code is performant and efficient, and you can catch performance regressions before they become a problem.

Conclusion

In this chapter, we've explored some of the best practices and idioms that have emerged in the Go community over the years. We've covered naming conventions, code organization and project structure, error handling best practices, and performance tips and tricks.

While these practices are not hard and fast rules, they represent the collective wisdom and experience of the Go community. By following these practices, you can write Go code that is more readable, maintainable, and idiomatic.

However, it's important to remember that these practices are not a substitute for good judgment and critical thinking. Every project is different, and what works well in one context may not work well in another. As a Go developer, it's important to understand these practices and to use them as a starting point, but also to be willing to adapt and innovate as needed.

Ultimately, the goal of these practices is to help you write better Go code and to be a more effective member of the Go community. By writing clear, idiomatic, and performant code, you can contribute to the success of your own projects and to the success of the Go ecosystem as a whole.

So go forth and write some awesome Go code! And remember, if you ever have questions or need help, the Go community is always here to support you.

Conclusion: The Go Community and Ecosystem

Throughout this book, we've explored the Go programming language in depth. We've learned about its syntax, its unique features, and its best practices. However, a language is more than just its technical specifications - it's also the community and ecosystem that surrounds it.

In this final chapter, we'll explore the Go community and ecosystem. We'll look at some of the most important libraries and frameworks in the Go ecosystem, discuss how to stay up-to-date with Go's evolution, explore how you can contribute to open source, and provide tips for connecting with other Gophers (as Go programmers are affectionately known).

Important Libraries and Frameworks

One of the strengths of Go is its rich ecosystem of libraries and frameworks. These tools can help you be more productive and write better code by providing pre-built solutions to common problems.

Here are some of the most important and widely-used libraries and frameworks in the Go ecosystem:

CONCLUSION: THE GO COMMUNITY AND ECOSYSTEM

Web Frameworks

- **Gin**: Gin is a lightweight web framework that focuses on performance and simplicity. It provides a minimal set of features and has a clean, expressive API.
- **Echo**: Echo is another lightweight web framework that aims to be fast and unfancy. It provides a simple, extensible core and a variety of middleware for common tasks.
- **Revel**: Revel is a more full-featured web framework that includes support for routing, templating, authentication, and more. It has a Rails-like MVC structure and aims to be productive and scalable.

Database Libraries

- **database/sql**: Go's standard library includes the database/sql package, which provides a generic interface for working with SQL databases. It supports a variety of drivers for different databases, including MySQL, PostgreSQL, and SQLite.
- **GORM**: GORM is an Object-Relational Mapping (ORM) library for Go. It provides a simple, idiomatic way to interact with databases using Go structs and methods.
- **MongoDB Driver**: The official MongoDB driver for Go provides a simple, efficient way to work with MongoDB databases from Go code.

Testing and Mocking

- **testing**: Go's standard library includes the testing package, which provides support for writing and running tests. It includes features like test functions, test tables, and coverage reporting.
- **testify**: Testify is a popular third-party library that provides a set of tools for writing expressive, readable tests. It includes features like assertions, mocking, and test suites.
- **gomock**: Gomock is a mocking framework for Go that generates mocks

from interfaces. It provides a simple, expressive way to create mocks for testing.

CLI and DevOps Tools

- **cobra**: Cobra is a library for creating powerful modern CLI applications. It provides a simple interface for defining commands, flags, and arguments, and includes features like help generation and shell completions.
- **viper**: Viper is a configuration solution for Go applications. It allows you to define configuration in a variety of formats (such as JSON, YAML, or environment variables) and provides a simple, unified API for accessing configuration values.
- **Docker SDK for Go**: The official Docker SDK for Go allows you to interact with the Docker API from your Go code. It provides a simple, idiomatic way to manage containers, images, networks, and more.

These are just a few examples of the many high-quality libraries and frameworks available in the Go ecosystem. By leveraging these tools, you can build powerful, reliable applications quickly and efficiently.

Staying Up-to-Date with Go's Evolution

Like any living language, Go is constantly evolving. New features are added, existing features are refined, and the ecosystem grows and changes over time.

As a Go developer, it's important to stay up-to-date with these changes. Here are some tips for doing so:

Attend Go Conferences and Meetups

Go has a vibrant conference and meetup scene, with events happening all around the world. Attending these events is a great way to learn about the latest developments in Go, meet other Gophers, and get inspired by the work that others are doing with the language.

Some of the most notable Go conferences include GopherCon (the largest Go conference in the world), dotGo (a European Go conference), and GoCon (a series of regional Go conferences).

By regularly reading these sources, you can stay informed about the latest developments in the Go community and pick up new tips and techniques for writing better Go code.

Contributing to Open Source

One of the best ways to deepen your understanding of Go and connect with the community is to contribute to open source projects.

Go has a strong culture of open source, with many of its core libraries and tools being developed openly on GitHub. Contributing to these projects can be a great way to gain experience, learn best practices, and give back to the community.

Here are some tips for getting started with open source contribution in Go:

Start Small

If you're new to open source contribution, it can be intimidating to dive into a large, complex project. Instead, start small. Look for projects that have issues labeled "good first issue" or "help wanted", or look for small bugs or improvements that you can tackle.

By starting small, you can gain experience and confidence, and gradually work your way up to larger contributions.

Read the Contribution Guidelines

Most open source projects have a set of guidelines for contributors. These typically include information about the project's coding style, testing requirements, and the process for submitting pull requests.

Before you start contributing to a project, be sure to read and follow these guidelines carefully. This will help ensure that your contributions are consistent with the project's standards and can be easily integrated.

Communicate with the Maintainers

Open source projects are typically maintained by a small group of volunteers. These maintainers are responsible for reviewing and merging contributions, as well as setting the overall direction of the project.

As a contributor, it's important to communicate with the maintainers. If you're unsure about how to approach a problem or have questions about the project, don't hesitate to reach out. Most maintainers are happy to help guide new contributors.

Be Patient and Persistent

Contributing to open source can be a slow process. It can take time for maintainers to review and merge your contributions, and there may be feedback or changes requested along the way.

Be patient and persistent. If your first contribution isn't accepted, don't get discouraged. Take the feedback you receive and use it to improve your future contributions. With time and practice, you'll become a valued member of the open source community.

Connecting with Other Gophers

Finally, one of the most rewarding aspects of being a part of the Go community is connecting with other Gophers. Whether you're seeking advice, looking for collaborators, or just want to chat about Go, there are many ways to connect with other Go developers.

Here are a few suggestions:

Join the Gophers Slack

The Gophers Slack is the primary chat platform for the Go community. It's a great place to ask questions, get help with problems, and chat with other Gophers.

Attend Local Go Meetups

As mentioned earlier, there are Go meetups in many cities around the world. Attending these meetups is a great way to meet other Go developers in your local area, learn about interesting projects and techniques, and build your network.

If there isn't a Go meetup in your area, consider starting one! The Go community is very supportive of new meetups, and you may be surprised at how many other Gophers are in your area.

By contributing to these projects, you can help make the Go community a better place for everyone, while also building relationships with other passionate Gophers.

Conclusion

In this chapter, we've explored the vibrant ecosystem and community that surrounds the Go programming language. We've looked at some of the key libraries and frameworks that make up the Go ecosystem, discussed strategies for staying up-to-date with Go's evolution, explored how to contribute to open source, and provided tips for connecting with other Gophers.

As we've seen, the Go community is a welcoming, supportive, and inclusive group of developers who are passionate about building great software. By engaging with this community, you can not only improve your own skills and knowledge, but also contribute to the growth and success of Go itself.

So whether you're a seasoned Go veteran or a newcomer to the language, I encourage you to get involved with the Go community. Attend a meetup, contribute to an open source project, join a discussion forum, or simply reach out to another Gopher for advice or collaboration. The more you engage with the community, the more you'll learn and grow as a Go developer.

And with that, we come to the end of our journey through the world of Go programming. I hope that this book has provided you with a solid foundation in the language, as well as an appreciation for its unique features, best practices, and ecosystem.

But remember, learning Go is just the beginning. The real journey starts now, as you take the knowledge and skills you've gained and apply them to your own projects and challenges. With Go's powerful features, rich ecosystem, and supportive community behind you, there's no limit to what you can achieve.

So go forth and build something great with Go! And always remember, whether you're a beginner or an expert, a solo coder or a team leader, you're a valued member of the Go community. We're all in this together, and we're all here to help each other succeed.

www.ingramcontent.com/pod-product-compliance
Lightning Source LLC
Chambersburg PA
CBHW050001230526
45465CB00003BB/1214